THE PARROT I

NEW ZEALAND
PARRAKEETS
(KAKARIKIS)

NEW ZEALAND PARRAKEETS (KAKARIKIS)

Dr JOSEPH BATTY

Beech Publishing House
7 Station Yard
Elsted Marsh
MIDHURST GU29 0JT

ISBN 9781-85736-2909
First published 1989
Second Edition 1997
Third Edition 2002
Fourth Edition 2007
Fifth Edition 2009

ISBN 9781-85- 36-435-4
CASED

A Catalogue entry for this book is at
the British Library

Beech Publishing House
7 Station Yard
Elsted Marsh
MIDHURST GU29 0JT

CONTENTS

PREFACE

KAKARIKIS are fascinating birds with behaviour which is not typically characteristic of parrakeets. They are curious birds which appear to like human companionship and thrive quite well in an aviary. They are not suitable subjects for a small cage.

They have had a chequered history, being slaughtered by farmers and hunters and then by rats and other predators. In addition, also in their natural habitat, they have had to contend with harsh conditions including cold and very wild weather.

Inevitably, this has taken its toll and a point was reached when they appeared doomed and would become, like the Dodo, an extinct species. In fact, they seemed destined for a worse fate because they were almost forgotten even by the people of New Zealand.

After a gap of many years enthusiastic breeders such as E. J. Boosey, the Marquess of Tavistock, and Sydney Porter tried to stimulate an interest in these birds. As a result, today they exist in quite reasonable numbers and appear to be all set for becoming one of the more popular species of parrakeets.

This book has been produced to stimulate further interest in New Zealand Parrakeets. In writing it I have consulted many books and journals. Comments and experiences of other breeders would be appreciated. The problem with a revival is that there are all too few articles or books on the subject in question. Unlike the keeping of budgerigars, canaries and other popular birds, time has been too short to establish the best practices.

In writing this concise book on the New Zealand Parrakeets I am mindful that difficulties exist on precise colours. Because some of the wild species have virtually disappeared and the domesticated species have been crossbred for colours there is no knowing what are the exact colours. One of the anomalies is that yellow-fronted have crimson-red frontal bands, but orange-fronted have an orange frontal area. In fact, in practice it may be reddish orange. All this is fairly academic because only yellow-and red-fronted appear to exist.

With Kakarikis common sense management appears to be the order of the day. Provide adequate shelter, a balanced diet and interesting surroundings and these birds will thrive and breed Experiment with fruit, green stuff and basic seed to see what they like.

Some fanciers feed daily, others give sufficient mixed seed for a few days and then supplement with fruit and greens on a regular basis. There is no hard and fast rule; so long as the birds are happy and thriving a flexible approach is acceptable. Overfeeding should also be avoided.

My thanks to Susan Lawson who photographed birds in colour.

J. Batty
June,1989

PREFACE (SECOND EDITION)

Much controversy greeted the first edition of this book including some criticism which was quite unjustified: Unfortunately in trying to cover a subject in a balanced and unbiased way it is difficult to suit everybody; there is a tendency for breeders to 'break out in a rash' and assert that methods advocated cannot be correct because it is not the way they have done it or been instructed by another breeder. Out of the many books I have written this became the most controversial in the United Kingdom; there has been no criticism from overseas.

In bringing out a new edition I have tried to add notes where appropriate, thus clearing up some of the points raised. However, whilst appreciating any constructive comments from fanciers, which are always dealt with, not all matters raised have been acted upon because no action was felt necessary.

The fact that a new edition is required is proof enough of the interest and appreciation shown . Regretfully let us face the facts that many of our armchair critics, with their moans and groans, do little to further the interests of our fascinating hobby; if they really could add to the literature and help fellow fanciers why do they hesitate. For the genuine fancier I leave the hope that each breeding season will bring joy and encouragement to carry on improving the Fancy and taking better care of our much loved . feathered friends.

PREFACE TO FIFTH EDITION

Interest in Kakarikis continues to grow — hence the new edition, but now hard backed because it is , after all, a reference book. Mutations are now established and and new mutations are being added. A Buttercup Yellow has been added to my small collection and the cock is unusually noisy. My thanks to those who assisted.

Good Wishes to all bird fanciers.

Joseph Batty

NORFOLK ISLAND
PARRAKEET

Yellow Fronted Kakariki

KAKARIKIS : NOMINATE SPECIES

Red
Fronted
Kakariki

Yellow
Fronted
Kakariki

Trestrail-McKenzie.

Two Basic Colours
From a painting.

CHAPTER 1
PARROTS AND PARROT-LIKE BIRDS
THE FAMILY GROUP

P ARROTS belong to the order *Psittaciformes* and are grouped into the family known as *Psittacidae*. Within this family there are different groups of species (around 330) which are further broken into around 60 genera.

A further classification is the division into sub-families such as:*

I. NESTORINAE -- covers the Kaka and Kea parrots from New Zealand.

2. STRIGOPINAE — includes the Owl Parrot or Kakapo.

3. CYCLOPSITTACINAE – a genus PSITTACULIROSTRIS which contains five species originating from New Guinea, dwarf-like (around 4 to 7 inches, 10 to 18cm) and believed to be related to the Lories.

4. PLATYCERCINAE -- which covers a wide range of species (29) which include the Rosellas.

5. CACATUINAE -- covers the cockatoos of which there are some 16 species. It includes the popular Cockatiels,

6. MICROPSITTINAE which includes six species of pygmy parrots. These diminutive birds (around 4in -- 10cm) which use their feathers to support themselves when climbing trees.

7. LORIINAE which includes around 60 species of brush tongued parrots known as Lories and Lorikeets which feed on liquids (nectars) rather than seeds.

8. PSITTACINAE — a group which contains the bulk of the parrots and range from quite small birds such as Love Birds to the Amazons, and the giant Macaws.

---

* This classification is not standardized so variations may be found.

Grey Parrot

Blue-fronted Amazon

Macaw

Ring-necked Parrakeet

Hooded Parrakeet

Rosy-faced Lovebird

Rose-breasted Cockatoo

Black-headed Caique

Species of Parrots

It will be seen that they range from quite small birds such as Love Birds to the giants such as Amazon and Macaw Parrots. The classification of a particular bird may be changed and it would then be included in its new group.

Because of the need to have an international language for describing birds Latin names are used, as well as the equivalent in the language of the country in which they are kept.

This can lead to rather complicated descriptions being used, but is obviously the only practical way.

PARROT FAMILY UNIQUE

Parrots and parrot-like birds possess features which are unique:

1. Beak which is hinged, the upper mandible being attached to the forehead in a manner which allows great movement and flexibility for cracking seeds and nuts.

2. Lower mandible is light, thin and deep which cuts into the foot. It is shorter than the upper, curved mandible.

3. Foot of the parrot is completely zygodactyle (two toes pointing forward and two back) and prehensile (capable of grasping), thus allowing great mobility, being able to climb vertical posts or trees, also using its beak in the process.

4. The fleshy tongue is thick and muscular and allows the bird to taste food and manipulate it within the beak, discarding husks or pods which are not eaten.

Obviously, this summary does not cover the multitude of varieties which exist. Special mention must be made of the Lories and Lorikeets which possess a tongue containing a brush of strong hairs used for procuring nectar food from flowers.

Yellow-fronted Kakariki in Aviary

CHAPTER 2
HISTORY OF THE *CYANORAMPHUS* PARRAKEETS

EARLY HISTORY

We are not always aware of the work done by aviculturists in preserving the New Zealand Parrakeet from extinction. Yet in these attractive Parrakeets we have a genus which has been brought "back to life" by the perseverance of a few dedicated bird keepers.

SETTING THE SCENE

Writing just over 55 years ago Sydney Porter, a much travelled aviculturist, wrote a series of articles in *The Aviculturist Magazine*. He explained the position with the *Cyanorhamphus*, as they are called, at that time, and parts of his work are now produced:

NOTES ON THE CYANORHAMPHUS* PARRAKEETS

The *Cyanorhamphus* Parrakeets form a very distinct genus and are confined to the New Zealand region; though some members are found on far distant islands which are no doubt the last remaining outposts of some vast continent which was submerged beneath the Southern Pacific Ocean many eons ago.

These Parrakeets vary in size from slightly larger than a Budgerigar, in the case of the New Zealand Alpine Parrakeet (*Cyanorhamphus malherbie*), to as large as a Pennant (Rosella Parrakeet) in *Cyanorhamphus cooki* from Norfolk Island, which is the largest of the genus.

Colour

In colour they are not particularly striking, being more or less of a uniform grass-green marked with either red or yellow, and blue. These Parrakeets are remarkable for the fact that they inhabit regions far from the tropics and several species are confined to desolate, bleak, and often treeless islands, where the species have become, owing to the absence of trees, practically terrestrial.

---

*Note the slightly different spelling from the modern version *Cyanoramphus.*

Unfortunately, civilized man has dealt very hardly with these birds and several species are now extinct; others are on the verge of extermination, while none are in a flourishing condition. The two commonest species, which were confined to the mainland and which were found in great abundance before the advent of the white man to the shores of New Zealand, are now greatly reduced in numbers and are found only in the most remote forested districts as well as on several of the islands off the coast.

The two species mentioned, the Red-fronted Parrakeets and the Yellow-fronted Parrakeets, were very well known to British aviculturists fifty* or more years ago, and were bred with comparative ease in the aviaries of several bird-keepers. But it was the same with these as with any other bird which was comparatively easy to obtain, people did not bother to breed them and they just died out. Now these interesting species will never grace our aviaries again.

THE ANTIPODES ISLAND PARRAKEET
(Cyanorhamphus unicolor)

This unique Parrakeet is confined to a tiny island far distant from New Zealand, and well on the way to the chill Antarctic Ocean. Very few specimens have been brought away alive. Buller , the great New Zealand naturalist, had several; the Zoological Society had one or two many years ago; in fact, the type was described from a bird in the possession of the Society, the habitat of which was then unknown, and recently the Marquess of Tavistock possessed a single example. This bird, which is doubtless the last which will ever reach these shores, was procured by a sailor from a small ship which stopped at the island.

The bird was knocked over with a stick by the man on the shore, which shows how fearless this species is in a wild state.

I had great hopes of visiting the lonely island which forms the home of this strange Parrakeet, for I thought that I might be able to get as a passenger on the small Government steamer which once a year visits the islands in the far south in search of castaways and also to replenish the food store on the islands which is kept in case any unfortunate individuals get shipwrecked there. But alas! I found out from the High Commissioner in London that, owing to means of economy, the steamer no longer visited the islands on the borders of the Antarctic, and the would-be castaways are now left to their fate !

---

*Editorial Note: Fortunately he was wrong! They are still in existence but only due to the dedication of pioneer breeders.

Every inquiry possible was made, and I found that the only means of getting there was to charter a special ship, which would have to be of a large tonnage owing to the tempestuous seas. The price asked was £500, which, needless to say, was quite beyond my means, so I reluctantly had to give up the project.

I very much regret to say that I fear the numbers of this bird have been greatly reduced by the members of a certain American expedition which has been ravaging the islands of the Pacific for several years and almost wiping out whole species of birds. This expedition collected many skins of this species, and from what I heard of the brutal slaughter by the members of the expedition of this isolated type its fate is certainly in the balance.

The death knell of various rare island species is certainly sounded when such expeditions as these pursue their depredations unchecked. Instead of assisting ornithological research they appear to be hampering it, at least for future generations. They have left such a name behind them that they will never be allowed to collect again in many of the British Islands, especially New Zealand.

During my visit to Steward Island and the outlying islands I saw something of the terrible seas of those parts, and it is little wonder that few ships ever call at the bleak islands in the far south. The great marvel is that a Parrot has been able to adapt itself to such severe conditions as prevail on the island on which it is found. As mentioned before, it is very unlikely that the bird will ever be seen alive again by aviculturists in Europe, for which the stopping of the Government steamer and the total closing of the seal-killing season there is no reason for any ship to brave the terrible gales which rage in those seas.

The Antipodes Island Parrakeet is completely terrestrial and lives on the ground amongst the tussock grass, feeding upon the seeds of the grass. The very boisterous winds have made flight almost impossible for this bird, and it is very feeble on the wing, though it can run and climb about the rocks with the greatest agility.

W R B Oliver

W.R.B.Oliver, who has seen the bird in its native haunts, tells us in his book *New Zealand Birds* that this Parrakeet "is a ground bird which walks and climbs but seldom takes wing. It is found among the tussocks and scrub and also on the rocks along the shore including the breeding places of the Penguins. It is quite fearless and makes a low chattering sound as it walks about. It breeds in holes in the thick matted bases of the grass tussocks".

The Antipodes Island

A short description of the home of this unique bird may be of interest, and the following is an extract from a letter from the High Commissioner of New Zealand in London:

"The Antipodes Islands lie some 490 miles east-south-east from the southern most point of Stewart Island. The largest island is known as Antipodes Island, and measures 4 miles from east to west and 2 miles from north to south. At its highest point it reaches an elevation of 1,300 feet. The coast is rocky and precipitous, with steep slopes covered with tussock rising from the tops of the cliffs to the high land in the centre of the island. The tussock grows from 4 to 6 feet in height in many parts and so close together that it is a matter of difficulty to force one's way through it. There are no trees on the island, but some patches of shrubs, particularly in the shallow gullies, where rank growth of fern are also found. In addition to the various seabirds which nest there, the island is noted for a small Green Parrakeet, which is found fairly plentifully amongst the tussock grass."

The weather on this isolated island is far from ideal, terrible gales and storms sweep over it in the winter time from the Antarctic which make it anything but a desirable place for a Parrakeet to live on. But in spite of this it seems to have been able to fight the elements and hold its own until the coming of the arch enemy of all feather life, Man, who seems to have made short work with this highly specialized and interesting species. The Antipodes Island Parrakeet is about 14 inches in length and of a uniform yellowish grass-green, with the primary coverts and the outer edges of the primaries bright blue. The legs are particularly long and eminently suited for the terrestrial life which the bird leads.

Some of these birds were transferred to Kapiti Island in 1907, but there were none there when I visited it. Highly specialized animals hardly ever thrive when transferred from their own habitat to another. There is certainly no tussocks on Kapiti on which the birds could feed.

Buller says: "My captive birds seemed perfectly happy although caged when adult. They partook freely of maize and oats, also of apples, grapes, figs, and, indeed, ripe fruit of any kind. They could bite severely, as I soon learned to my cost. .. Although captured as adult birds they readily take to confinement and do not fret, as most other birds do, at being caged. I have noticed that this species has a habit of resting at night in an upright position, holding on to the wires of its cage by both bill and feet."

THE MACQUARIE ISLAND PARRAKEET (Cyanorhamphus n.
erythrotis)

Macquarie Island will no doubt be better known to readers as the original "Penguin Island". It is one of those tiny islands which lie far off the coast of New Zealand and well on the way to the Antarctic. It was until recently the scene of the most terrible and disgusting slaughter of the Penguins, when every year tens of thousands of these hapless birds were driven into great vats or digesters to be boiled down alive for the sake of a cheap commercial oil used mainly for the greasing of ropes, as it was a trifle less in cost than mineral oil.

On this island lived a small Parrakeet of the *Cyanorhamphus* group, a bird like the Antipodes Island Parrakeet, which was particularly terrestrial in its habits, more from force of circumstances than anything else, as there are no trees on the island, it being too bleak and wind-swept. This Parrakeet, like the last, derived its sustenance from the seeds of the tussock grass and also nested under the clumps of the same grass. A scientific expedition which called at this island within recent years failed to find the bird,so had reluctantly to come to the conclusion that it was extinct.

Some time afterwards I met one of the professional Penguin killers from Macquarie Island, and he told me that the Parrakeet had disappeared prior to his advent there some years before the War. There is little doubt that this bird was exterminated through the agency of cats, which were brought by the Penguin killers in the very early days and which were left to fend for themselves when the men left in the winter. These animals have greatly increased and still take a great toll of the bird life. The Macquarie Island Parrakeet is similar to the Red-fronted Parrakeet, but is of a more yellowish green, especially on the under parts, and there is very little blue on the wings.

THE RED-FRONTED PARRAKEET
(Cyanorhamphus novaezelandiae)

There is no doubt that in the course of time both this bird and its ally, the Yellow-fronted Parrakeet, will vanish from the mainland of New Zealand. Fortunately it will not vanish from the face of the earth so long as the New Zealand Government still retain the Little Barrier Island, Kapiti Island, and the islands off Stewart Island as sanctuaries for New Zealand's much persecuted, bird life.

On these islands the birds are numerous, especially the Red-fronted. The latter birds are also extremely common on some more very small islands, the names of which had perhaps better not be mentioned.

Once exceedingly common, the Red-fronted Parrakeets were to be seen in flocks of thousands; now on the mainland they are restricted to a few very remote localities. On my arrival in New Zealand I spent a considerable time in searching for these birds, and at last tracked down a small colony in the forest reserve of Lake Waikaremoana. In every other locality I was told that the Parrakeets were very plentiful forty years or more ago, but had now quite disappeared and were now never seen.

Like most of New Zealand's birds, it is dependent on the forests for its food, and it is intolerant of any interference on the part of man. For wherever timber-felling operations are started prior to the burning of the forest, the birds quickly disappear. Many years ago Parrot shooting was a favourite "sport" with the colonists, and this no doubt helped to reduce the numerical strength of the birds to a great degree.

This Parrakeet is very rarely kept in captivity in New Zealand now. When I was first in New Zealand I did hear of one, but when I tracked it down it proved to be a White Cockatoo! We shall never see this interesting species in our aviaries again, except perhaps an odd one or two now and again which happens to be smuggled out of the country , for the New Zealand Government would rather see fifty perish in a forest fire than a single pair leave the country for breeding purposes.

To show the great rarity of this bird on the mainland, many people who were interested in birds had never seen it and most ordinary people had never even heard of it. The birds which I did manage to see on the mainland were exceedingly timid and it was impossible to get within a good many hundred yards of them, except once in the forest at Takahue, when one alighted near to us, but as soon as it became aware of our presence it was off like a shot from a gun.

On the little Barrier Reef Island this Parrakeet finds sanctuary and it is extremely common; in fact, I should think that the Parrot population of Little Barrier is greater than that of the entire mainland. On first setting foot on that fascinating island the Parrakeets were the first birds which attracted attention. What a joy it was to see these brightly coloured birds only a few feet away instead of a quarter of a mile away as I had done on the mainland. Here they were utterly fearless, and my first "birdy", thrill after landing. was to see one of these birds only a few feet away feeding on the seeds of the native flax which grew on the beech.

The favourite diet of the Parrakeets is the seeds of this plant *(Phormium)*, known locally as "flax", but bears no resemblance to the plant known as flax in Europe. The seed pods are like small hard bananas and are borne in clusters in a candelabra-like fashion on stems which grow from 10 to 15 feet high. Each pod is packed with peculiar flattened black seeds, the kernel of which in the centre is white and nut-like to the taste. By the time the pods are ripe one finds that nearly all have been torn to pieces by the Parrakeets.

I endeavoured to procure a quantity of these seeds for my Norfolk Island Parrakeets, which would also doubtless feed on them, since the plant is found on Norfolk Island. As all the seeds were eaten as soon as they ripened by the Parrakeets, I plucked a huge stock of the partly ripe seed pods and placed them under bushes covered with branches of trees, hoping that they would ripen in that way. But on arriving at my treasure store some days later to collect the seed I found that I had been outwitted by the Parrakeets, who had discovered my hoard and systematically opened every pod.

Around the caretaker's house on the island the birds were comparatively tame, coming down to feed on the various seeds in the garden and also on the apples which they seemed to relish in a half- ripe state. It was when in the apple trees that we were able to approach nearest to the birds, usually within two or three yards.

On a small group of islands which we visited we found the Parrakeets very plentiful; on one of the very smallest islands they were especially numerous. These islands are very small, and although they were covered with the densest vegetation it was amazing that they supported such a large Parrot population. Most of the islands were almost inaccessible except the one where the Parrakeets were so plentiful, and access to this was only gained through climbing up a precipitous and partly dried-up waterfall. During the rainy season it would be quite impossible to gain access to this island at all. It is doubtless the inaccessibility of these islands which has saved the Parrakeets.

The season had been very dry and there were only one or two small pools on rocky ledges, and these formed the sole drinking places for the birds on the island. All manner of native birds were perfectly tame; the Parrakeets came round and settled within a foot or two of one; in fact, they seemed to ignore the presence of human beings, treating us as though we were non-existent. I have seen few birds as tame in a wild state as the Parrakeets on this island. A professional bird, catcher could have caught hundreds in a morning. I spent two days and one night there, sleeping under the shelter of a huge "flax" like plant on the beach so that I could observe the habits of the birds at their drinking places early in the morning. In this I was disappointed, for I found that the best time for seeing the Parrakeets was in the heat of the day, when there was a constant stream of them coming to drink and bathe. It was on this island that I heard for the first time the very distinctive goat-like bleat of these birds which caused the Germans to call this species "Ziegensittich".   At first I thought there must be numerous kinds in the bush as there are on many of the small islands off the coast, but I soon found out the noise was made by the Parrakeets.

On the first three of the chain of islands which we visited the "flax" plants were entirely stripped of their seeds, and on these islands the Parrakeets were not nearly as plentiful as on the last island, where there was still a large quantity of seed, so it is obvious that the birds pass from one island to another as the supply of seeds runs short. There must be a considerable shortage of seed in the winter time, for I cannot think what the birds would eat except the hard seeds of a pampas-like grass called in the vernacular "toi-toi". I spent a good many hours watching the Parrakeets at their drinking place and noticed that some of the birds seemed to prefer to settle on the perpendicular rocks and suck up the moisture which oozed through the cracks. I noted, too, that the birds were extremely agile in their movements on the rocks, running up perpendicular faces with the utmost ease.

On another fairly large island some miles away from the small group mentioned above we found the Parrakeets fairly numerous, but not nearly as tame as on the former islands. We were fortunate in finding a nest of almost fully fledged young ones within 2 feet of the ground. This nest was in a hollow puriri tree and the three youngsters could easily be reached by the hand. During the time my hand was inserted in the nest it got covered with tiny lice-like insects; when I withdrew it it was covered with a brown crawling mass of these creatures. Whether they came off the birds themselves or from the rotten wood I do not know, but it must certainly have been very uncomfortable for the birds. The youngsters were exact replicas of their parents except that the cere was very large, occupying quite half of the beak.

I understood from other naturalists that the Parrakeets were also very common on another small group of treeless islands to the north of New Zealand. These islands we intended to visit but did not do so. This was a matter of great regret to me, as I understood that owing to the absence of trees the birds were ground- nesting.

Distribution Map of Kakarikis

It is almost impossible to get hold of any of the *Cyanoramphus* Parrakeets now in New Zealand. On the mainland the birds are so scarce and wary that no one is able to catch them. Then there are no bird trappers, for all birds are protected and it is against the law to own any native birds except Keas and Zosterops. Even were it possible to get hold of any it would be impossible to get Government permission to export them out of the country.

All the islands I have mentioned are bird sanctuaries, where all bird life is rigidly preserved and Government permission is needed to visit them. This is, of course, as it should be, for no one wants to think of the unique avifauna of New Zealand becoming extinct. But so long as the islands are protected the If the New Zealand Government paid as much atterition to the wicked and wanton burning of forests, with its terrible toll of bird life, which goes on every where unchecked, as it does to the slight moral lapses of some of its citizens, it would earn the thanks of posterity birds will be safe from extinction. The only fear now is from the increase of cats and rats upon the island and from forest fires. It has been known for cruising parties to land on the islands and deliberately set fire to the forest during dry weather .

Buller says, in writing of this species in the second edition of his work, published in 1888: "It is quite the cottagers' friend in New Zealand. Riding or driving through the suburbs of the provincial towns -- Porirua and Karori districts, for example, near Wellington -- you will notice in many of the farmers' houses and roadside cottages small wooden cages of primitive construction (often merely a candlebox or whisky-case, faced with wire-netting or thin bars) fixed up to the front of the building or under the simple verandah. On closer inspection each of these cages will be found to contain a tame Parrakeet --the pet of the rustic home and 'Pretty Poll' of the family. I have often been quite impressed at fmding how attached these simple people become to their little captive. Now all is changed, for, search as I would from one end of the country to the other in my endeavour to obtain examples of this Parrakeet, I found only four examples in captivity, and these belonged to two naturalists who kept them and did not wish to part with them. Most New Zealanders do not know that a Parrakeet ever existed in their country, so rare is this bird to-day on the mainland.

THE YELLOW-FRONTED PARRAKEET *(Cyanorhamphus auriceps)*

Rare as the Red-fronted Parrakeet is, this bird is far rarer. It is almost unknown on the mainland of New Zealand, though in the middle of the last century it was even commoner than the other bird, appearing in flocks of countless numbers and devouring the corn and fruit of the settlers.

The first time we met with this rare bird in a state of freedom was on the little Barrier Island. It will always stand out as one of the "red-letter" days of my life, for it was on that day we climbed Mount Archeria, the highest peak in the centre of the island. The island looked so sinister and foreboding as we approached it that I little dreamed of being able to stand on the top of its inaccessible-looking peak. But it proved easier than it looked. The climb was one of the most interesting I have ever done; up to 500 feet the way lay through dense manuka-bush, which is a secondary growth, replacing the burnt forest, until after that the way lay through virgin forest of mixed growth until,   at about 1,000 feet, this changed to kauri forest, there being many magnificent specimens of this giant forest tree. At about 2,000 feet this changed into semi-alpine rain forest. Here it was a veritable fantastic fairyland, stranger than was ever pictured in the imagination of man. Everywhere seemed a fantastic mixture of trees, rocks, ferns, and mosses. In some places, strange as it may sound, it was like a fairy cavern where it was impossible to tell which was the ground, the rocks, or the trees. From the top it was possible to see the whole island, running in precipitous forest-covered ridges from the sea to the culminating point in the centre.

On the summit one stood in the clear rarified atmosphere in the brilliant sunshine, far above the rolling white mist clouds which the currents of air wove into strange wraith-like shapes. It was here that one realized the true significance of the beautiful Maori name "Hauturu", meaning "the resting place of the winds of Heaven".

It was at a height of about 2,000 feet that we first heard the chattering of Parrakeets, but it was a different note from that made by the Red-fronted, a softer and more melodious sound. I realized almost at once that it was the call of the Yellow-fronted Parrakeeet from the sound I had heard of a captive bird. But try as we would it was impossible to see the birds; the green of the plumage harmonized so well with that of the trees that in the dim light of the forest it was impossible to distinguish the birds. Fortunately on the way down, not far from the summit, a pair of Parrakeets flew down into a low sapling only a few feet away. Once, to my surprise, it proved to be a Yellow-fronted and the other a Red-fronted. It almost looked as though these were a pair , though this would be impossible. I watched the bird which I took to be the hen for about a quarter of an hour; she was quite tame and appeared to take quite as much interest in me as I took in her.

This delightful Parrakeet was at one time, fifty-odd years ago, quite common in English aviaries, but has, alas! grown scarcer and scarcer until at last it is practically extinct in the North Island, the little Barrier Island being one of the few places where it is found today, and even there it is far from common. This is strange, for it is supposed to be a very prolific breeder; Gutherie Smith records having found nine young ones in a nest.

The Yellow-fronted Parrakeet is now almost unknown in captivity in its native land, for apart from its rarity it is an offence against the law to keep it. I only came across two birds in my travels, both males, and I am quite sure these were the only ones in captivity. There is no more charming bird in existence from an aviculturist's point of view than this dainty and intelligent little Parrakeet. It is very beautiful, friendly, easy to feed, has no harsh notes, does not destroy woodwork, and is altogether the most delightful bird one could wish for. In the old days it was quite easily bred. It is a thousand pities that a small breeding stock could not be available for it soon adapts itself to captivity. Twenty years ago a Mr Bills of Dunedin brought a hundred or more of them in cages to England, and they found ready purchasers at a guinea each. What would such a consignment be worth to-day?

I made a special trip down to Stewart Island, intending to visit some of the small outlying islands off the South Cape, mainly Mogg Island, Evening Island, and Hidden Island, where this Parrakeet is reported to be still found in considerable numbers. The Fates were against us. We set out in a 50 ft. yacht, but the tempestuous seas proved too much for our small craft. For nearly a week we battled with the gales, having to seek, often enough, shelter in the wonderful inlets off the coast of Stewart Island. What a relief it used to be to find refuge in these quiet and beautiful waters which gave no indication of the fury outside! They were real havens of refuge, where we could light a fire and thaw our frozen limbs and get something to eat. Eventually, so bad did the seas become that we stood no earthly chance of ever arriving at our destination, so reluctantly we had to turn stern about and let the gale blow us back to safe anchorage in Half Moon Bay.

How these delicate-looking little Parrakeets manage to survive on these small islands, which for four or five months of the year are swept by bitter winds from the Antarctic, I do not know. The climate, by all account, resembles that of the West Coast of Scotland. But this bird, like so many others in New Zealand, seems to have been successful in adapting itself to its environment, for it is very evident that no member of the Parrot family could originally evolve under such adverse conditions.

I visited Ulva's Island in quest of this bird, but failed to find it, though I have no doubt that it was there, but our stays on the island were of very short duration and we had little time to make a thorough search of the dense forest. Unlike the Red-fronted Parrakeet, this bird does not seem to find any of its food in the open, and I have never seen it on the flax plants. It seems, more or less, to feed upon the fruits of the forest trees.

Buller says: " At irregular periods after intervals of from seven to ten years this Parrakeet (in company with the preceding species) visits the settled and cultivated districts in astonishing numbers, swarming into the gardens and fields, devouring every kind of soft fruit, nibbling off the tender shoots on the orchard trees and eating up the pulse and grain in all directions. The last of these visitations occurred in the early part of 1886 and the one before that was at the close of 1877." Now all is changed, the Parrakeets have gone, never to return, and few are New Zealanders who have been fortunate enough to catch even a glimpse of this bird within recent years.

THE CHATHAM ISLAND PARRAKEET *(Cyanorhamphus forbesi)*

While the Red-fronted Parrakeet has many forms and sub- species found on far outlying islands, even as far as the Society Islands, the Yelow-fronted species has (or had) but one ally, namely Forbes or the Chatham Island Parrakeet. I should use the past tense for this bird has now joined the many species of the *Cyanorhamphus* group which have been exterminated by human agency, The extinction of this rare Parrakeet was directly brought about by a well-known ornithologist in this country, who years ago had agents in the Chathams collecting large series of skins of the various island species, many of which inhabited islands of only a few square miles. The Parrakeet soon disappeared and a party of scientists who had been over there recently failed to find it at all even though they made an extensive search. And all we have is a few perishable skins now transferred to America.

There are no records of the wild life of this bird so, like the Alpine Parrakeet, its history is now a closed book.

THE ALPINE PARRAKEET *(Cyanorhamphus malherbei)*

Try as I might, I was unable to trace anything about this dainty little Parrakeet. After travelling about in the various districts where it was found and by questioning many people who should have known it, I reluctantly came to the conclusion that if not actually on the verge of extinction it must be excessively rare. In the Southern Alps, its original habitat, it seemed to be quite unknown to anyone there. The only recent data concerning it was a fresh skin received at the Auckland Museum from the Nelson District. There is little doubt that in a few years' time this species will become extinct, for it is not found on any of the island sanctuaries, though it was reported to have been found on the Little Barrier Island and on the Hen Island. This was in the middle of the last century. It is certainly not found there now, though why it would become extinct, when its two congenitors are still found there, I do not know.

Buller in his *Birds of New Zealand* says of this bird, "In its native haunts it may be found frequenting the alpine scrub, in pairs or small parties, and is very tame and fearless. It is by no means uncommon in the wooded hills surrounding Nelson. At Nelson I saw many caged birds of this species, and one in particular was remarkable for the clear manner in which it articulated the words "Pretty Dick", repeating them all day long in the most untiring way ."

Fifty or more years ago it was very occasionally imported into this country, but was never bred here, although there is a record of some young ones being reared in France in 1883 .This unobtrusive little bird seems to have been known but for a few years, twenty or thirty at the most, and to have passed on, regretted only by those of us who deplore the wanton and wasteful destruction of Nature's most finished products. At the present rate another two or three hundred years will see the end of nearly all feathered life on this globe of ours, unless Man providentially manages, with the aid of poison gas, etc., to exterminate him self.

Looking through much literature I have been unable to find anything concerning this bird in captivity , and no one I met in New Zealand had either kept it or seen it alive, so its history now appears to be a closed book.

THE SOCIETY ISLAND PARRAKEET *(Cyanorhamphus nealandicus)*

Only three species of the *Cyanoramphus* Parrakeets were found in islands lying within the tropics and far from the typical habitat of this group of birds. The Society Islands are a group of small and remote islands lying almost midway between Australia and South America. The species was first made known by Captain Cook, who first visited the island in the eighteenth century .Not long after the settling in the islands of the white traders the Parrakeet commenced to disappear and nearly fifty years ago it was reported as extinct, only two specimens being known. It was one of the few Parrakeets in this family which had a juvenile plumage.

The adult bird differed rather from most of the family. In colour, the forehead was black, a stripe through the eye and also the rump feathers being scarlet, the flight feathers blue and the rest of the body a bright green.

THE ULIETEA ISLAND PARRAKEET (*Cyanorhamphus ulietanus*)

Like the last-mentioned Parrakeet, this species is also extinct. It was confined to one small island in the Society Group and was reported extinct over a hundred years ago. This bird differed from all the other members of the family by having the plumage an olive brown colour, the head brownish black, the rump and basal upper tail coverts brownish red, the under parts olive yellow. It was the most distinctive in colouring of all the Cyanorhamphus Parrakeets. Nothing is known of its habits and only one or two skins are in existence.

THE LORD HOWE ISLAND PARRAKEET (*Cyanorhamphus subflavinscens*)

A Parrakeet very closely resembling the Norfolk Island Parrakeet (*Cyanorhamphus cooki*) was once plentiful on Lord Howe Island, but soon after the island was colonized by the white races the extermination of this Parrakeet began. It was shot, no doubt, by the settlers owing to its feeding upon the growing corn. This bird has now been extinct for between thirty and forty years. It was slightly smaller than C. *cooki,* but resembled it in colouring. It is sad to think that of the fifteen known species of this family no less than six are now extinct and the others, with the exception of the Red-fronted Parrakeet which is only numerous on certain small islands, are on the verge of extinction.

THE KERMADEC ISLAND PARRAKEET *(Cyanorhamphus n. cyanurus)*

A matter of between five and six hundred miles to the north. east of New Zealand lie a group of small islands known as the Kermadecs, which until recent years were inhabited by a single family who raised sheep on one of the largest islands, namely Sunday Island. Finding that, with the slump in wool prices, farming on these lonely islands was not a commercial proposition, the family left and, I believe, the islands are now left to their original inhabitants, the birds, before the advent of man to this lonely spot a small Parrakeet of the *Cyanorhamphus* group was exceedingly plentiful, in fact it still is on some of the small outlying islands, where cats and rats have not been introduced. Where these pests have found a home on the larger islands the ranks of the Parrakeets have been sadly thinned out.

I had the good fortune whilst in New Zealand to see a true pair of these very rare Parrakeets, which were in the possession of a gentleman who had been on an expedition to the islands and had managed to secure this pair of birds. The hen was nesting, sitting I believe on eight eggs in a hollowed-out tree trunk in her small aviary. This, I understood, was the second time the birds had laid, the first time laying eight eggs which proved infertile. I left before the result of the second clutch was known. The birds were in rather cramped quarters and it was hardly to be wondered at that the eggs were infertile. The owner said he was going to re-wire a large aviary, occupied by Peafowl, with small mesh wire, so that the Parrakeets could be turned into it and thus have a better chance of breeding. It is to be hoped that this is done, for a brood of these rare birds would be a great acquisition from an aviculturist's point of view.

Though similar to the better known Red.fronted Parrakeet this bird differs in several points. It is larger, the wings and tail are a much brighter blue and the cheeks are a bright emerald green, also they struck me as being a different shape; for one thing the head appeared to be smaller and the neck much thicker. The red spot on the back is larger than in the Red-fronted, the hen can also be more easily told from the cock by her differently shaped head. The owner of the birds, who, as previously mentioned had been to the Kermadecs, told me that the Parrakeets were very plentiful on the smaller islands but were very rare on Sunday Island -- the one where the sheep farm had been. They nested in crevices in the ground and fed mainly on grass seed.

The birds referred to were in very fine condition, being fed mainly on natural food with little seed, the hen of the pair was not the original one, she having died of egg binding after laying twenty eggs.

A pair of these birds were imported into this country a few years ago, having been presented to the late Governor who, when he retired, brought them back to Great Britain, and for all I know they may still be here.

If this chapter happens to meet with the eye of the owner of the birds in New Zealand perhaps he will be good enough to send us a little more information about them, which I am sure would be very welcome, as so little seems to be known of these exceedingly rare birds.

There is only one skin of this bird in the British Museum and that was obtained from Raoul Island.

CHAPTER 3
FIRST BREEDING RE-COMMENCED

KESTON BIRD FARM

In the mid-1930s breeding of the Yellow Fronted Parrakeet was restarted. Without that action being taken there is little doubt that members of the genus would have been lost. The instigator appears to have been the doyen of foreign bird enthusiasts E.J. Boosey who, with his partner, ran the Keston Foreign Bird Farm. He recorded his experiences in *The Foreigner* a bi-monthly magazine issued by his company.

Much of what he states applies. equally today and therefore an edited version is reproduced below:

HOW TO BREED THE YELLOW-FRONTED NEW ZEALAND PARRAKEET *(Cyanoramphus auriceps)*

Owing to their rarity and the strict laws that prohibit their export from New Zealand and the neighbouring islands, the *Cyanoramphus* Parrakeets are nowadays practically unknown to aviculture.

Many years ago, one member of the genus -the Red-fronted New Zealand seems to have been fairly extensively kept and to have had the reputation of being an extremely prolific breeder. *Cyanoramphus auriceps,* the subject of this chapter, is now probably the rarest of the family and shares with the Alpine Parrakeet, C. *malherbi,* has the distinction of being the smallest member of the whole group, being only 9.6 inches long or about the size of a Bourke's or a Blue-winged Grass Parrakeet.

Their prevailing colour is a rich, rather dark moss-green paler on the breast, a band above the beak and a patch on the flanks bright red, fore-part of the crown golden-yellow; some blue on the lower edge of the wings; bill a pretty silver, shading to black at the tip. The eyes are very striking, owing to their brilliant ruby red irides.

One great advantage they possess is the ease with which they may be sexed, the hens being not only less brightly coloured, but a good two sizes smaller than their mates, so that it is quite possible to tell them apart at a glance even from some distance away. So marked is this distinction that it reminds one more of the difference existing between the size of the sexes of certain of the Raptorials, such as the Sparrow-hawk, though in their case, of course, it is the hen who is the larger. Though, as will be seen, they are by no means gaudily coloured, yet I think their really remarkable tameness, intelligence, and vivacity would-cause anyone who had ever been lucky ennugh to possess a pair, to rank them very high indeed on their list of favourites. If someone suddenly hit upon the bright idea of holding a *concours d'elegance* of Parrakeets, and if, furthermore, I happened to be the individual chosen for the invidious task of placing the entrants in their order of merit, I should; at any rate, have one compensation -- the awarding of the first prize would be easy. I should give it without hesitation to the Princess of Wales, that rare and lovely Parrakeet from Australia which nature has seen fit to endow with what one cannot help thinking is a good deal more than its fair share of beauty of form and charm of disposition. But the awarding of the second prize would be more difficult; yet, if general attractiveness of character and intelligence ranked high and brilliance of plumage were a secondary consideration, 1 think 1 know on which of two birds my choice would fall. It would be either Bourke's Parrakeet or the subject of this article.

If Yellow-fronted New Zealands will not, as does a Princess of Wales, greet one with shrill screams of delight as soon as one goes near their aviary, they will nevertheless become even more lively than usual, just to show you how pleased they are to see you. When you get quite close to their aviary, they will hop on to the wire netting, perhaps rather high up, and then -- a thing which few other Parrakeets ever do -- they will run rapidly *downwards* until on a level with your face. They then subject you to a careful bright-eyed scrutiny, after which they will probably fly down on to the ground, the whole manoeuvre being typical of.all their actions, which I think are best described as a "hop, skip and a jump."

Once on *terra firma* they execute several long jumps, varied with short hops, after which they settle down to a minute examination of the earthen floor of their flight. This process is most amusing, and I shouldn't like to say how many precious hours I've wasted, watching them.

First of all, the pair will walk about side by side, scratching in the soil occasionally with their long legs after the manner of poultry (Incidentally, no other group of Parrakeets have this purely gallinaceous habit). Then one of them, perhaps the cock, will come across what he considers to be a particularly intriguing stone or small lump of earth. Instantly, his mate will rush up to him to be, as it were, "in at the kill"; but he usually has other ideas on the subject, and all she gets is a firm, yet gentle, push in the face from her husband's outstretched foot, and she generally takes the hint and goes off prospecting on her own.

Parts of Keston Foreign Bird Farm

Left to himself, her husband examines his find at his leisure. First of all, it is pushed aside to see if anything of interest lies beneath it; then, in one foot -- though he uses if far more as if it were a hand - -he will pick up the object of his interest -- be it a leaf or a stone or merely a piece of earth -- and turning it first this way, then that, subject it to the most careful examination.

Sometimes this takes a considerable time, but usually he is able to decide at once that it is unworthy of further attention, and throwing it aside, goes off after his wife, who being similarly employed, dismisses her husband with as liltle ceremony as he had employed to her, namely a determined push in the face.

Soon after this, both will fly up into their aviary, after which a bout of extreme activity ensues, both of them hopping, flying and jumping so quickly that their separate movements are difficult to follow. I have devoted more space than usual to a description of the birds' actions and general behaviour in an aviary, because it is in these, and in their curious voices that all the *Cyanoramphus* Parrakeets differ so utterly from any other group. When one first hears their cry , one imagines a small Parrakeet to be the very last possible source from which it could have emanated. It is, in fact, exactly like the bleating of a sheep heard from some distance away. However unattractive and monotonous this may sound in print, it is entirely saved from being either through the bird's habit of varying the tone and *tempo* to suit its moods. Sometimes it is rather slow and grave. At others it sounds light- hearted and gay, being higher-pitched and much more quickly reiterated. Then again, there is an intermediate, slightly absent-minded, meditative note which they often employ when engaging in their absorbing pastime of treasure-hunting, which I have already described.

Cock *Cyanoramphus* Parrakeets are *reputed* to be liable to murder their wives at any moment, and without the slightest provocation. Personally, I am inclined to doubt this, and it certainly does not apply to'the Yellow-fronted, though it may to some of the larger members of the genus, such as the Norfolk Island, which has a much more powerful beak.

Yellow-fronts are very willing to go to nest, and hens are quite easily suited with a nest box. The six young ones bred here at Keston last season from one pair were reared in a wooden box, with a hole near the top, about 18ins. deep by 7ins. square, containing a few inches of earth on top of which an inverted square of turf had been placed, the box being hung vertically under slight over-head shelter in the open flight. It was rather late in the season, when by a stroke of luck we were able to obtain a proper husband for the hen, who had originally, as a make-shift, been mated in April to

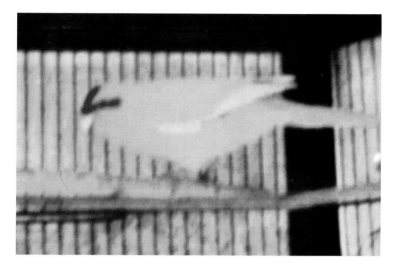

Buttercup Yelllow Cock

Green Mutations

Yellow Fronted Kakariki (side view)

Red Fronted Kakariki

Red-fronted Kakariki
Note red spot behind the eye.

Kakariki lacking blue pigment (omitted in printing) thus showing how Yellow and its variations are produced.

a cock Blue-wing their four eggs proving unfertile. When introduced to the cock Yellow-front, however, she immediately went to nest again, laying a clutch of six eggs, all of which were successfully hatched and reared.

During all this time she was left severely alone and we were only made aware that a brood had hatched by the curious cry of the young ones being fed in the nest, which is just as distinctive as their parents' sheep-like bleating, and resembles nothing so much as the far-off, high-pitched screaming of swifts as they wheel in wide circles on a summer evening.

Yellow-fronts are not difficult to feed, but they need careful rationing, particularly of such oily seeds as hemp and sunflower. Their staple seed mixture should consist of one part canary, one part white millet, quarter part brown millet, quarter part oats, with a very small pinch of hemp, and *not* more than a dozen grains of sunflower per day to each bird: The latter seed, particularly seems in any considerable quantity to upset their *digestions*. They should be given a continuous supply of millet spray and fresh sweet apples, not only when they have young ones to feed, but the whole year round.

When they have a brood to cater for, a few handfuls of their ordinary seed should be thrown daily to sprout on a mound of earth, or preferably peat-moss, in the open flight. The amounts of hemp and sunflower can both be gradually increased until, just before the young ones are due to leave the nest, the parents are being given two handfuls of sunflower and one of hemp thrown on their mound morning and evening, in addition to canary and oats and millet. At all times they are great green-food eaters, and particularly appreciate a freshly-cut square of turf, which is a useful way of providing them with green food during the winter months. Not only will they eat the grass, but tear the turf to pieces, eating the root as well.

During the breeding season they should be given, besides turf, as many spinach-beet leaves as they will eat. A Mr. Bouskill, who reared them about forty years ago, and who seems, besides our-selves, to have been the only other aviculturist ever to have bred the Yellow-fronted New Zealand in England, recommends numerous mealworms as part of their diet; of this I can only say that none of those we have here will touch them. This, however, is probably only another of those cases one so often encounters of individual preference among birds of the same species, and I should certainly imagine that mealworms, in moderation, would be a wholesome addition to their diet if they could be induced to take them.

Typical Red-Fronted Kakariki

This shows the normal bold carriage of the species, always curious and friendly, but watch carefully because at first opportunity they will escape from the aviary, but after a spell of freedom will want to get back.

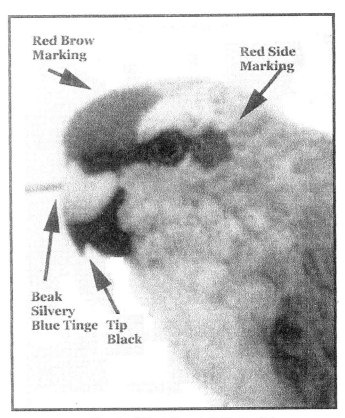

Red Brow
Marking

Red Side
Marking

Beak
Silvery
Blue Tinge Tip
Black

Head of Red-Fronted Kakariki
The detail of the different species is given in Chapter 4

Yellow-fronts have only one real failing as aviary birds, and that is they cannot be considered entirely hardy. This is the more extraordinary as their native climate is anything but genial, since, at any rate in winter, they have to put up with high winds and a decidedly lower temperature; in addition to frequent fogs. Yet, in this country, they are far more susceptible to our unpleasant winter weather-- which incidentally must be so very like their own -- than, for example, the Hooded Parrakeet, which hails from tropical northern Australia, yet will winter out of doors in an unheated aviary without so much as turning a hair, however bitter the weather may be.

Judging by our experience, therefore, Yellow-fronts are far best kept in a roomy flight.cage in a warm bird-room from the beginning of October to the middle of April.

FOOTNOTE: Comments on Mr Boosey's Contribution:

I. Scratching This trait has been observed by one or two breeders and certainly appears to be in accordance with the natural behaviour of birds in the wild (see Mr Porter's comments early in this chapter) but the author has found that some birds in captivity do not scratch. Possibly the fashion to provide concrete floors in aviaries has eliminated the urge in some species. My own birds scratch constantly.

2. Aggressiveness The experience of non-aggressiveness has been recorded by many breeders. Through careful selection over many years the unpleasant trait may have been bred out. Sydney Porter *(ibid)* states how friendly and tame they are in the wild and this is still the same in captivity. However, as all experienced bird fanciers know birds which are friendly and extrovert can turn and become quite vicious, particularly in the breeding season. Our experience tends to suggest that generally Kakarikis are free from vice.

3. Nest Boxes Selection of the most appropriate nest boxes is very important. If too small ehicks are squashed and, if too large, eggs get scattered.

4. Whether Hardy Again opinions differ. Many breeders regard Kakirikis as being quite hardy. It would appear though that 50 years on they are more hardy than indicated by Mr Boosey. Nevertheless, for those with a bird house an internal flight may be an advantage for those winter months when frost and snow prevail.

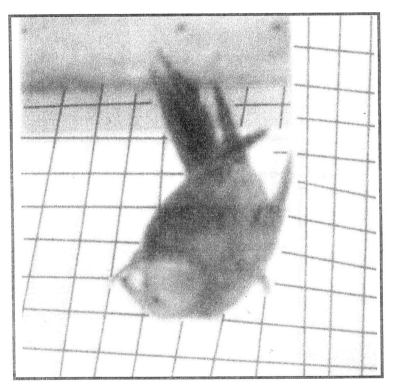

Acrobat on Wire
Kakarikis are very athletic and run up and down the wire of the aviary.

MORE RECENT VIEWS

More recent findings on *Cyanoramphus* are now summarised. For more detailed information readers are referred to *The Parrots of the World*, Joseph M. Forshaw, 1972 and subsequent editions:

1. Red-Fronted Parrakeets (8 sub-species). These are now rare birds, but can be found on the outer islands such as Little Barrier Island, Auckland Islands and Antipodes Island.

2. Yellow-Fronted Parrakeets (2 sub-species). After a positive falling off in numbers they are mutliplying in the forest regions. Forshaw suggests they are tree-dwellers to a greater extent than the Red-Fronted Parrakeets which tend to rely on ground cover .

3. Orange-Fronted Parrakeet. This Parrakeet continues to be very rare and as a result very little is known of its habits , or feeding details. Apparently it has been sighted on rare occasions, the last recording being about 20 years ago.

Forshaw suggests an orange frontal band for this bird, , but the painting by W T Cooper in *The Parrots of the World* shows what could be a crimson band (possibly reddy-orange), very little different from the Yellow-Fronted Parrakeet shown on the same illustration. This anomaly is commented on by the author in the descriptions of the birds in Chapter 4. Unfortunately, because of the rarity of the Orange-Fronted Parrakeet, there is no way of checking whether the frontal area of the head should be, red or orange.

Significantly the Yellow-Fronted frontal band is reddish and, therefore, it would appear that the illustration by Cooper is correct. Presumably the original genus had a red frontal area and the other two are variations. Possibly the Red-Fronted Parrakeet is the nominate race and the other two are mutations. There is no evidence to support this statement, but if seems more likely for colours to come lighter than to come darker. The experience of the author in colour breeding with various birds has been that darker colours are more difficult to maintain, whereas pigmentation losses tend to occur fairly easily.

Over the years breeding has continued so that Red, Yellow, and Orange Fronted Kakarikis are available. There are well-founded grounds for suggesting that purity of blood and colour are open to doubt. Hybrids have been produced which are not strictly in accordance with the descriptions of species found in the wild.

The fact remains that these, delightful birds have been snatched back from extinction and we are now able to enjoy their companionship.

FOOTNOTE -- NORFOLK ISLAND PARRAKEET.

As this book went to press for the first edition came news that *Cyanoramphus n. Cooki* had been bred in captivity on Norfolk Island by staff of the staff of the Australian National Parks and Wildlife Services.

Norfolk Island Parrakeet
Now very rare, although captive breeding is now reviving the species.

CHAPTER 4
NEW ZEALAND PARRAKEETS IN AVICULTURE

DISTRIBUTION

These distinctive parrakeets originate from New Zealand and the surrounding small islands where in Victorian times they were regarded as a social and economic menace creating havoc rather like a plague of locusts. The farmers reacted violently and, as a result, they were exterminated in large quantities.

The Red-fronted Parrakeet is now a protected species in New Zealand . Some of these birds live quite near to the South Pole, so obviously they are quite hardy. In any event they breed quite easily in captivity so for all practical purposes they are fully domesticated in the UK and other countries. (See Distribution Map)

ORIGIN OF NAME

In popular usage for some time now the description Kakariki is generally accepted for a generic term to identify these parrakeets. How the name originated is not always understood. Two versions are given by different writers:

(a) From the sound of their cry; kiki ;

(b) Based on the Maori language, simply meaning a small parrot.

The latter interpretation probably represents the more acceptable meaning.

TEMPERAMENT WITH OTHER BIRDS

Most breeders of Kakarikis* suggest that they are of equable temperament, being friendly and agreeable with other species. This has been our experience.

Breeders in the past have had problems, usually a "rogue" cock who kills his wife and others who are introduced into the aviary .This behaviour is recorded by the Marquess of Tavistock *(Parrots and Parrot-Like Birds)* who cites the birds kept by a Canon Dutton not only killed their companions but also ate them!

---

*The plural may be spelt as "Kakariki', "Kakarikies', or as adopted in this book.

The fact remains that like many other species of Parrakeet -- especially at breeding times -- they do tend to be aggressive and have to be watched. If in doubt with a particular cock or hen it is wise to clip *one* wing, thus rendering him less mobile. Any other birds, can then escape from bullying. However, this is a step which is best avoided because it spoils the birds and reduces the enjoyment of seeing them fly around. In any event, follow the normal practice of keeping one pair of Kakarikis only in an aviary and this reduces the chance of conflict.

These will normally be quite agreeable to other types of birds in the aviary. The author has kept doves, budgerigars and even cockatiels with Kakarikis without problem.

The conclusion must be that usually Kakarikis are agreeable together and quite friendly with other genera and care should be taken to ensure that harmony prevails.

BEHAVIOUR WITH BIRD-KEEPERS

Kakarikis are friendly characters who become quite docile. If watched through the aviary wire they will come quite close and are very tame. They run up the wire or up the sides of the aviary and generally behave in ways which are quite different from that displayed by other Parrakeets, being constantly on the move. They will run along a ledge and then fly to a perch and back again.

There is no set pattern to their behaviour and this makes them very interesting to watch. If a dark corner or ledge is available they will perch there. The author has an overhanging roof and the kakarikis insist on going to roost in the dark recess even though perches and parts of bushes are available for perching. The Budgerigars in the same aviary keep to the conventional roosting places.

When attending to chores in the bird-room there is no panic from the Kakarikis. They will fly around, but not with the wildness found with some types of birds. They are even tamer than their aviary companions, the Budgerigars. They are not known for their talking abilities but they can be taught and this adds to their interest as aviary birds.

Unusually for Parrakeets, they do not chew everything in sight. They therefore do not require any preventive measures to perches or other wooden features in the aviary.

CONCLUSION

Kakirikis have much to recommend them on the following grounds:

1. Colourful

2. Apparently intelligent and inquisitive and they appear to like domesticity

3. Lively and unpredictable in behaviour

4. Generally live in harmony

5. Fairly easy to breed *

6. Require standard Parrakeet-type foods which present no problems

7. Do not destroy wooden nest boxes and aviaries

Accordingly, they can be recommended as ideal birds for the aviary where they will give many hours of enjoyment to the bird keeper . Against them is the occasional problem from a rebel cock bird when he has to be watched. This does not seem widespread. In addition, some breeders have alleged a relative short life in an aviary, possibly only a few years reported by some bird keepers, but it is difficult to generalize on the longevity. In othe words, this is not a general finding so there must be a reason for some failures; this may be incorrect feeding, over exposure to the weather resulting in chills, or bad management. They must have adequate space for flying and a covered shed for relaxing in and they should then retain their health and vitality for many years.

---

*The experiences of at least two breeders suggest that Kakarikis prefer an aviary and as little disturbance as possible or eggs may be neglected or broken. (See *Parrot Society Magazine* Vol.XII, No.11, Nov.1978, where W. Hardy relates his experiences when keeping Kakarikis in a large wooden cage. The five eggs were broken by the birds.

THE SPECIES EXPLAINED

There is some difficulty in giving precise descriptions of the main species, which are very similar. The distinguishing features are connected with the head :

a) Brow band (deep crimson red or reddish-orange)

b) Upper head band (red, yellow or orange).

It is the colour of these two which determines the precise species although, in practice, they have been interbred to such an extent that they may be difficult to find in their exactly pure form. However, this should not be exaggerated because the author has visited different bird fanciers and seen Red-Fronted Parrakeets as well as Yellows.

According to I.S. Dyer *(Kakariki)* many of the so called Orange and Yellow Fronted Kakarikis are hybrids and possess a patch behind the eyes which should be on the Red Fronted Species only. *

In fact, it seems likely from the experiences of the different breeders that the modern Orange Fronted birds are really crosses, possibly from the Yellows and Reds.

DESCRIPTIONS : NEW ZEALAND PARRAKEETS OR KAKARIKIS

1. **Red Fronted Parrakeets**
2. **Yellow Fronted Parrakeets**
3. **Orange Fronted Parrakeets**
4. **Cinnamon (a new colour mutation)**
5. **Various Other Mutations; eg, Pied and Lutino.**

---

*Readers are referred to the Magazine of the Parrot Society for January and February 1989 for a feature by G. Carss and a reply by Mr I. S. Dyer on the dangers of Cross-breeding the different colours.

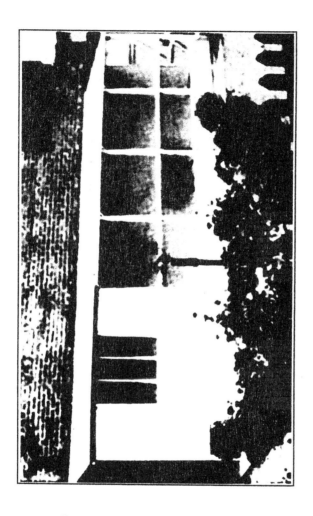

Lean-to Aviary with Flight Combined

Markings of Kakariki

Red frontal band on Yellow Fronted and on Red Fronted, but fully red on the latter.

Orange Fronted is in between Yellow and Red Fronted.

RED FRONTED

The Red Fronted are known as *Cyanoramphus novaezelandiae*, and there are supposed to be nine races, although the bird keeper need not worry too much about that fact. In the wild many races have disappeared altogether so obviously the aviculturist must view those in existence as being of importance.

The fact that races or sub-species existed and may still exist can be of considerable interest to the ornithologist, but there is no way of distinguishing captive stock as being one race or another this being dependent on the original source of other species.

YELLOW FRONTED

The Yellow Fronted (two sub-species) come under the same name *Cyanoramphus*, but with the addition of *auriceps* to show the variation.

As stated earlier, they are part of the Parrot Family known as *Psittacinae*. The name of the race *Cyanoramphus* refers to the bill or beak which is cyan; ie, Blue. In fact the beak is a grey-blue with a black tip, but when the sunlight shines on it, different colours may be seen, sometimes almost like mother-of-pearl. .

ORANGE FRONTED

The Orange Fronted is known as *Cyanoramphus Malherbi* and may exist in New Zealand, but is rarely seen in captivity, although hybrids may appear to be this species.

OTHER DETAILS

Size: Around 10 inches long (25cm) to about 12 inches (30cm)
The Yellow and Orange Fronted tend to be at least 1 inch smaller. In all species the females are smaller than the matching male, again by 1 inch (2.54cm) or a little more.

The Kakariki is a medium sized bird with no exaggerated features. Unlike many other parrots the head does not appear large and there is very little indentation between the back of the head and the shoulders; ie, the neck.

The tail is quite long and when viewed sideways appears to represent about half the overall length.

As noted, females are smaller in length; they also tend to have smaller heads and beaks.

Colour: Body, Rich darkish green With an intermingling of yellow on some species. The Red Fronted is usually regarded as being darker in colour with less yellow, but many Yellow Fronted are also quite dark in the body.

Wings: Rich dark blue on the wings viewed when the bird is perched, ie on the outer flight feathers.

Tail: Broad and swallow-shaped and of a vivid grass green colour with a tinging of yellow and dark shading on some parts.

Head: Since the head determines the species it follows that great attention should be paid to this aspect,

Brow: The brow is red in both Yellow-Fronted and Red- Fronted birds with an orange colour in Orange-Fronted Kakarikis. It will be .noted that the Yellow-Fronted Parrakeet has a reddish brow, yet logically this should be yellow. In the Orange-Fronted the brow is a bright orange or reddish-orange. and the skull is a yellowish colour. A similar (colour exists for the Yellow-Fronted Kakarikis) although many descriptions specify that the upper head should be an orange colour ,

Red-Fronted Side Bands: The Red-Fronted Parrakeets have distinct side pieces extending from the base of the beak to behind the eye and it is the latter patch which is found only in pure Red species including related species such as *(Cyanoramphus cooki.)*

Eyes: The overall impression of the eyes is dark brown with a bright red iris, They are full of expression and alertness,

Legs: The legs are a browny colour and appear slender and long, except when the kakariki is walking or sitting when they will be hidden by the plentiful feathering which is a characteristic ot the genus.

MUTATIONS

Mutations have now been bred which is a lucrative trade for those who breed for profit, the new colours fetching high prices. Sometimes, the standard form is lost altogether, which is a great pity. However, mutations are quite attractive and do stimulate interest. Details are given later in this chapter.

NOTES ON KAKARIKIS

More experience has been acquired on these attractive Parrakeets. This may be divided into a number of areas:

1. Breeding
2. Introduction of more Mutations.

BREEDING

There is now acknowledgement that Kakarikis, when healthy, well fed and housed correctly, will breed quite regularly. In fact, some pairs have nested a number of times each year, records existing to show that as many as four clutches may be incubated and reared in a 12 -month period. In fact, the hen may be so keen that she will start another nest before the young are fully weaned and independent. If this occurs the male bird should take over and feed the chicks.

Generally bird keepers would try to limit the number of clutches to two in a year, controlling by removing the nest box. The young birds may pair up at 5 -6 months old, but are better when more mature and steady, a year old being the minimum starting age. Breeding can then continue for a number of years.

Incubation appears to vary, but 18 - 21 days is the range. The female broods, starting to sit after laying two eggs. The chicks are then fed for 6 weeks when they should leave the nest and, in 2 -3 weeks, should be able to fend for them selves, possibly being placed in a separate aviary if accommodation permits. The average clutch is around 6 eggs, but as many as ten may be laid.

When hatched the chicks have white down which changes to grey. The birds can be distinguished by size, the male bird being large than the female.Courtship by the cock is rather dramatic. He jumps around and bows and weaves. He also feeds the hen and, when a nest box is placed in the aviary he goes through the entrance hole, showing her where she can nest. She will then look inside, but it may be some days before laying commences.

Nest boxes should be fairly deep with a short perch inside the pop hole and a flat 'ladder' secured to the inside for easy access. The base should be filled with peat moss or compost which is naturally damp and wood shavings placed over the top to allow the eggs to be kept clean. The dampness of the base, up to 3inches (about 8 cm) in depth ensures there is adequate moisture for hatching the eggs.

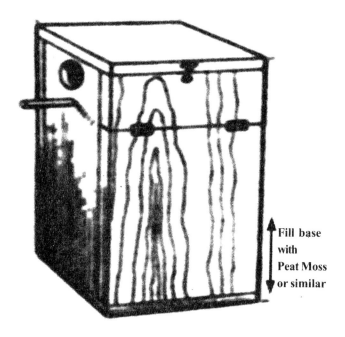

Fill base
with
Peat Moss
or similar

Grandfather Clock Nest Box
Ideal for Kakarikis

MUTATIONS

Because of their many advantages over other parrot-type birds Kakarikis are now very popular. Much of the uncertainty of breeding is avoided and they are attractive and easy to manage.

The mutations available and possible new mutations are covered a little later. It is interesting to note that these birds sell for a fairly high price so there is an incentive to breed them.

Whether it is a result of the crossing to develop the mutations is not clear, but they do appear to be full of vigour. Also, in the last two decades, size appears to have increased in some strains, making them more attractive.

Kakariki Mutations Have Increased Tremendously
See Text

BASIC GENETICS
DETERMINATION OF SEX

The Phenotype of the off-spring is determined by the genes which the young bird inherited from its parents, and similar remarks apply to the determination of its sex.

In genetics, the chromosomes are described diagramatically as X and Y. The chromosomes of the male, so far as sex determination are concerned, are both of the X type. The female carries one X and one Y chromosome, the Y chromosome being the determining factor in the reproduction of female young.

When the new sex cells are being formed, the chromosomes split and travel to opposite sides of the new cells. In the male, both new cells will carry an X chromosome, but in the female, one new cell will carry an X chromosome and the other will carry the female Y chromosome.

COCK'S CHROMOSOME   **HEN'S CHROMOSOME**

Chromosomes in Birds
The female determines the sex of the young.

If a male cell then comes into contact with an X-carrying cell from the hen, the resulting chick will be male. If the chromosome which carries the X factor from the male comes into contact with a cell carrying a Y factor chromosome from the hen, the resulting chick will be female.

Reference to breeding with *Sex Linkage* is mentioned in connection with Cinnamons and Lutinos. With the former there may be some doubt whether the colour is truly Cinnamon because other colours also appear in the plumage, but with Lutinos there can be no doubt because the vivid yellow is quite positive.

SPLITS

The term "split" is used to denote a condition where a pair of genes do not match up, although a non-standard colour is present. Thus in Kakarikis the normal colour is green, but if the paired structure (the chromosomes) do not match, although green will still be the colour, there is hidden colour such as yellow which may appear in its pure form when both genes carry the yellow.

Both genes being identical is referred to as *homozygous;* i.e, same colour. Where they differ they are *heterozygous* and would be described as, *for example:*

Split—Green/Blue.

This means the bird is carrying a Blue gene and may produce some Blues. In practice, a very long wait may be experienced before the elusive new colour appears; sometimes it never occurs.

COLOUR MUTATIONS

In the space of two decades the number of mutations has grown considerably. In fact, the normal Red- and Yellow-Fronted are becoming rather scarce which would be a great pity if these were neglected.

The possible colours are as follows:

1. Red-fronted Kakariki
(Cyanoramphus novaezlandiae)

   (a) Cinnamon

   (b) Pied (Recessive)

   (c) Pied Dominant)

   (d) Lutino

2. Yellow-fronted Kakariki
(Cyanoramphus auriceps)

   Lutino

RED-FRONTED CINNAMON

Cinnamon is a difficult colour because it is often found with other colours in the plumage. No doubt it is affected by the nominate species from which it was bred. Thus, in the case of cockatiels the cinnamon colour is quite recognizable, being a yellowish-brown with a tint of light grey. However, with Kakarikis, at present, the breast is yellow tinged with green, the tail is cinnamon, whereas the back is greenish with cinnamon markings. In other words, at present, many specimens are not truly, and fully, cinnamon as seen by an observer.

The guide to whether a bird is the true colour is to check whether there is black or positive grey in the plumage; the existence of either shows it is not a true Cinnamon. The Cinnamon may also have a plum coloured eye (reddy), although, since others may have this eye colour, it is not an absolute guide. Ground colour is also a guide because the Cinnamon ground colour is yellow, but, when dealing with fawn, the ground colour is white.

Another essential in breeding Cinnamons is there should be sex linkage. A hen has one chromosome (X) which is operational and carries certain genes, as well as Y which is too small to carry genes, but the cock bird has two chromosomes (X). When mated together the result may be the Cinnamon colour which is visible or, if not apparent, the offspring may be split for the colour.

Matings for Cinnamon have been suggested, each having the colour in at least one side of the mating:

CIN X NORMAL Hen = Normal/CIN COCKS
+ CIN hens

CIN X NORMAL Cock = Normal/CIN COCKS
+ CIN hens

CIN Cock X CIN Hen = Cinnamon Cocks & Hens in the ra-
tion of 50 : 50.

Other possibilities could be given. The results will be divided, depending on the matings. Thus a Cinnamon cock X Normal hen is likely to reproduce Cinnamon hens plus Splits cocks in the ratio of

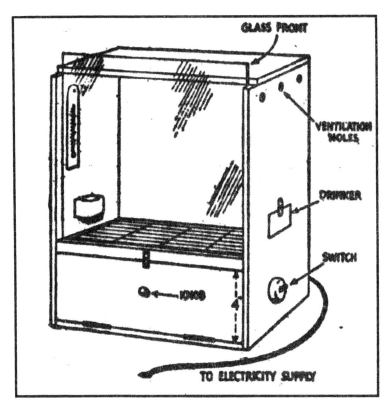

Hospital Cage or Rearing Box

50 : 50. But a Split cock X Cinnamon hen is likely to produce 25 per cent of each -- Normal, Split, Cinnamon cocks, Cinnamon hens.

Mating Normal male and female together will not usually produce any Cinnamon varieties, unless, accidentally a mutation (a 'Sport') is produced. This would then be bred back, possibly to a parent or other member of the same family in an effort to establish the new Mutation. Only when a number have been produced can it be said that the new sub-species has been established.

RED-FRONTED PIED (RECESSIVE & DOMINANT)

Pied is the name given where there is a mixture of colours, occuring in patches. In some respects the markings are quite haphazard, with patches of different colours appearing on the yellow. At present the ground colour is yellow, but theoretically another base colour could appear.

Colours on the Pied birds may be green, blue, and some dark colour such as intermediate black. The red patches would also be present.

If possible the markings should be evenly distributed which looks better than an uneven spread. Sometimes Pied birds have yellow heads, whereas others have green heads and, whilst this does not detract from the fact that they are Pied, even marking looks better. Through selection for colour it should be possible to breed birds that are evenly marked.

Pied may be Recessive with the result that offspring may be split for colour, so the pied content is not always apparent. However, Dominant Pied also exist and can be bred quite easily once birds with the dominant gene are owned. Results will vary when using Normal birds which are mated with the Pied. There is a Double Factor gene or a Single Factor gene and which one exists will affect the results in breeding.

Suggested formulae for the **DOMINANT** Pied are as follows:

Pied Double Factor X Normal = Single Factor Dominant 100%

Pied Single Factor X Normal = SF Dominant + Normal: 50 :50

Pied SF X **Pied SF** = 50% SF; 25% DF: 25% Normal.

Pied SF X **Pied DF** = DF & SF : 50 50. (ie, equal numbers)

Recessive Pied

The position and exact genetic makeup of the Recessive Pied is not straight forward. Also, in some cases it has been reported that there has been an interaction with the Pied of the Red-fronted Kakariki. This has resulted in two different Pied mutations being developed named Golden Yellow and Gold Checked*. There is not a great deal of information on these possible mutations.

The main difference between the Recessive and Dominant appears to be the stability and colour, the former showing other colours such as pied patches. In addition, there are likely to be offspring which are Splits, the Pied colour not visible.

Whether the Recessive Pied do appear in the Red-fronted Kakariki is uncertain and therefore it would appear that the suggested formulae above would still apply, but substituting **Recessive** for **Dominant**.

---

* **Reported in** Colour Mutations & Genetics in Parrots, **Dr. Terry Martin, 2002, Australia, which is an excellent guide to the complex world of colour mutations.**

RED -FRONTED LUTINO

The Lutino is a beautiful Canary Yellow which is, in effect, a form of Albino because it has pink eyes. The colour comes from a sex linked recessive gene.

Sexed Linked

If a male Lutino is mated to a Normal female the offspring should be females Lutino and males Green. On average there should be 50 per cent males and 50 per cent females, but this is unlikely to occur in individual hatches, so a number of nests will have to be taken together for the statistical average to work out.

A male, having two sex chromosomes, may have Lutino linked to one or both; i.e. split when linked to one and a visible mutation when linked to both.

The female does not have two sex chromosomes and therefore is either Green or Lutino, whichever factor is linked to the single chromosome. It follows that the hen will not be a split Lutino.

Possible Matchings

1. **Lutino cock x Lutino hen = LC + LH (50:50)**
2. **Lutino cock x Normal hen = LCN (Split) + LH (50:50)**
3. **Split cock x Lutino hen = LC + LH + SC + NH (25% of each)**
4. **Split cock x Normal hen = LH + NH + SC + NC (25% of each)**
5. **Normal cock x Lutino hen = SC (Normal) + NH (No Lutions)**

In planning a breeding programme for maximising on Lutinos it will be necessary to take the pairings which are likely to give the most yellows. Thus:

Lutino cock x Lutino hen = all Lutinos
Lutino cock x Normal hen = 50% Lutino females
Split cock x Lutino hen = 25% Lutino males + 25% Lutino females

MEANING OF MATING FORMULAE

This summary of possible mating expections is much simplified. Unfortunately, we are not always aware of the background of many of the birds used for breeding.

Our "mutation" may be a single breeding, a "freak", never to be reproduced again. The so-called *Splits* may have little chance of producing the colour believed to be carried.

Any one with experience of colour breeding will know that unrelated strains may produce all kinds of results from colours hidden away for generations. This *atavism* or *reversion* brings about many surprises. Despite what is sometimes suggested, the breeding of different colour mutations is *not* an exact science and the problems are immense.

OTHER POSSIBILITIES

Much more experince and mutation breeding has occurred with Ring
Neck Parrakeets* and, since the basic colour of the Normal birds is
green, it follows that the Mutations developed for Ring Necks may be
possibilities for Kararikis. These have been listed and are as follows.
However, other colours are still appearing.

They may be as follows and others are reported on a regular
basis:

> 1. **Grey (now well established), Grey/Blue, Slaty;
> Pastel Grey).**
> 2. **Olive (called Grey-Green in Britain).**
> 3. **Cinnamon.**
> 4. **Turquoise Blue.**
> 5. **Deep Yellow.**
> 6. **Pied.**
> 7. **Deep Blue/Mauve; Violet.**
> 8. **White— Yellow or Blue Bred. *See* also Creamino.**
> 9. **Cinnamon Blue.**
> 10. **Silver.**
> 11. **Mixed Colours; eg, Grey/Green; Pastel Blue
> (blue with green on shoulders).**
> 12. **Lime (Lacewing); Green on yellow ground colour.**
> 13. **Dilute.**
> 14. **Fallow.**
> 15. **Khaki (also known as Misty).**
> 16. **Opaline.**
> 17. **Creamino (Albino/Yellow).**

---

* See *Ring-Necked Parrakeets*, Joseph Batty, BPH, 2003.

DIFFERENCES IN DEFINITIONS

Opinions differ on what each colour really represents. When does a "fallow" become an "olive"? What is a "Lutino" and when does this become a "deep yellow" or "primrose"?

In the "off colours" a wide variety of permutations may be possible. There may be a yellow head on a green or blue body.

Another possibility would be an inter-mingling of colours. This is different from a Pied which usually takes the form of a mixture of colours in distinct sections. This alternative may take the form of a "splashed" bird when colours appear in an haphazard fashion, without any form of regular marking.

The number of mutations is now confusing and bewildering and some form of classification is needed to simplify and not be exact on colours that appear very occasionally. Those that are established should be defined within clear parameters so that birds with some known colour, eg, cinnamon, should not have too much of any other colour, otherwise it becomes a different category.

64

Red Fronted Kakariki

CHAPTER 5

ACCOMMODATION

KEEPING PARRAKEETS

ADEQUATE SPACE ESSENTIAL

PARRAKEETS may be kept in cages or aviaries, but, if the former, it is usually stressed that the cages should be as large as possible so that the birds can exercise. They are constantly on the move and to limit them within small cages appears rather cruel. Filled with curiosity in any aviary, the birds run or fly from one part to another, constantly exploring so very restricted space will simply not suffice.

Some have the habit of feeding on the ground and Kakarikis even scratch like poultry, a habit to be considered when planning the housing, and obviously cages cannot provide the necessary conditions for their natural habits.

With all birds in captivity the aim should be to make the environment as near as possible to natural conditions. Parrakeets come from remote areas, feeding on berries and insects and nesting in hollow trees or rocks. What could be more unnatural than a cage!

LIFE IN CAPTIVITY

The appropriate conditions; ie, adequate space and fresh air with protection from the inclement weather and predators are vital for keeping and breeding any Parrakeets. An aviary is usually essential, covered with wire mesh for the flight.

Wire Mesh

Parrots and Parrot-like birds require fairly strong netting which may be :

1. Conventional wire-netting

2. Weld mesh which has perfectly joined squares or rectangles giving a neat appearance.

There is a tendency to use light weld mesh these days although in fact wire netting is quite adequate and may be cheaper. The thickness should be appropriate for the birds being kept, thus:

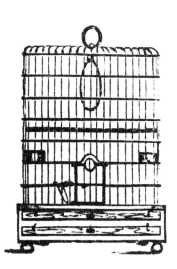

PARROT CAGES

These are still in use, but are quite cruel and should never be used for the larger parrots which require space for flying.

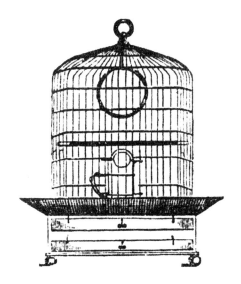

Parrakeets
0.50 x 0.50 inch (12mm) 16 wire guage thick
Parrots
1 inch x 1 inch (25mm) and 12 guage thick.

Remember it is also desirable to keep wild birds out of the aviary so a small size is preferable, but note the cost rises dramatically when the smaller sizes are used.

GENERAL PRINCIPLES

Housing Parrots and Parrakeets in appropriate cages or aviaries is of vital importance to their health and well-being. If breeding is to be attempted, conditions must be excellent or efforts will be wasted.

The fancier's choice will be influenced by what he can afford. Some modem breeders are prepared to sacrifice a great deal to build a purpose-made aviary of brick with windows and ventilation. In the long run such expenditure may well be justified, but many fanciers manage very well with home made sheds and flights.

Cages may serve many purposes -housing, breeding, showing, or training. They may be kept in a room in a dwelling house for the pet bird or in a bird room specially made for the purpose. The use of small open cages has long been the subject of criticism; they are only suitable where there are no draughts.

There is now legal recognition that birds should not be kept in small show-type cages for long periods. They are too restricting and, therefore, not recommended for a permanent home. Obviously a cage-bird like a parrot should have a very large cage.

CAGES

The types of cages found in use are as follows:

1. Domestic Fancy Cages for use in the home.
These are usually pleasing in design and hang on stands or rest on a small table. For the enthusiast with money to spend on antiques there are some splendid cages which will do justice to the most discerning householder. However, they can be very generous in space with many compartments. For parrots, very strong cages are essential with thick wire.

2. Breeding Cages which may have one or more compartments -- single, double or treble. Basically they are wooden boxes with wire fronts. They enable the birds to have privacy; the smaller type are unsuitable for parrots which would

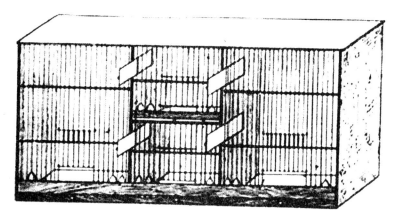

Double Cage
Not usually suitable for breeding.

Small Indoor Aviary

be restricted and chew through the wood.

3. Small-Indoor Flights & Similar for Outside.

If a suitable place can be found, these can be a feature of the house. A friend who lived in a converted coach house had the flight and living quarters for the birds in a entrance hall downstairs, which was seen on entering the house to go upstairs to the living quarters; downstairs there were stables which housed poultry and Jack Russell dogs. However, such an arrangement is not for everybody and many house wives cannot stand birds indoors.

There are now many metal aviaries available which can be used indoors or outside, although for the latter they should be adapted to provide shelter from inclement weather. Height is important because an avaiary approaching 2 metres high gives quite a good distance for flying upwards from the floor and from perch to perch.

An octagonal structure or similar of the height mentioned can fit into a small garden without difficulty and can be quite attractive.

Those with plenty of space can elect to have a larger flight area, especially for Ring Necks and Conures, when the can fly from one end to the other. A good length allows plenty of exercise, whereas a great is not as important for these larger, active birds.

Some Parrakeets do not seem to like too large an area. Kakarikis, Turquoisines, Splendids, Bourkes and similar breeds are quite happy too live in a small aviary, but must not be overcrowded or contain too many species with the result that no one type can live in comfort. Mixed collections can be feasible, but no matter how these are selected there are bound to be problems. such as disagreements of nest boxes.

4. Nursery Cages for rearing youngsters when feather pecking and bullying takes place. This would not apply if birds are kept in aviaries. Some cages are fixed to the side of the aviary so the young birds do not feel isolated` from their parents.

5. Show Cages which may be the open wire type or box cages. The specialist clubs lay down the precise cage to be used for each breed and these must be used in accordance with the regulations of the particular club.

The statutory requirements are laid down by the various acts in existence in the UK and in other countries.

AVIARIES*

The design of the aviary is of great importance and therefore time should be taken to make sure the best structure possible is made or obtained. This can be attractive as well as functional and, in a garden, landscaping is very appropriate. Lawns, bushes, rustic fences, trellis work and other gardening features all help to create the correct environment.

Reference should also be made to the preceding section on indoor cages and aviaries.

FUNCTIONAL REQUIREMENTS

Factors to consider when designing an aviary are as follows:

1. Size of house or sleeping shed

2. Flights including covered section

3. Insulation and ventilation

4. Lighting

5. Protection from disease and predators

6. Perches and related equipment

7. Safety porches

8. Landscaping and Aesthetic Requirements

As noted earlier, the needs of the birds should be considered. Some like a large aviary with plenty of flying space: Ring-Necks come into this category, but others, like Kakarikis, thrive and breed in a smaller area, although allowance must be given for them to fly upwards as well as across, with plenty of perches. They are constantly on the move, for ever going to the floor, and the flying back to an upper perch. For that reaon a fairly high aviary is desirable.

---

* See *Aviaries —A Practical Handbook*, Joseph Batty, BPH.

The functional requirements cover the essentials for sound management and good health. These can be achieved in a solid building made of corrugated tin, but the impression can be one of make-shift economy which is possibly fine for a smallholding, but not for beautiful birds in a garden.

Both wooden and metal structures may be purchased which are pleasing in design. They can be adapted with internal partitions as well as being insulated.

Larger buildings are available in the form of stables or dog kennels and, again, they may be adapted for breeding rooms or indoor aviaries. They are usually of very solid construction and whilst costly they lend themselves to modification without difficulty. They are likely to suit the breeder who wishes to keep and breed a considerable number of birds.

SIZE OF AVIARIES

There is no hard and fast rule on the optimum size aviary. Usually, though, a minimum size of floor space of 1 square foot (30cm) per bird is taken as a guide (with the larger parrots requiring twice as much), but to allow for breeding around 1 square metre per bird is desirable. At the end of each season the space should be reviewed for young birds hatched can soon cause overcrowding.

A view often expressed is that cubic capacity should not be taken as a guide to the size of aviary required. Whilst this may be the case it is also true that the extent of the flights attached to aviaries will be important in determining whether birds have adequate room. If they are flying around or perching on the flights they will be relieving pressure on the aviary proper (the sleeping apartment).

CONSTRUCTION

Today there are many excellent sheds available from the local garden and bird centres. There are also many very poor structures. Very thin board affixed with wire staples will not last; nor will it give adequate protection to the birds. Avoid such sheds because in the long run the apparent cheapness will prove to be very expensive.

Essentials are as follows:
1. Solid timber preferably lined with some form of insulating board {not soft material which the birds can peck away). Tongue and grooved boarding is very desirable because this avoids draughts. Usually 3/4 inch board (around 30mm)

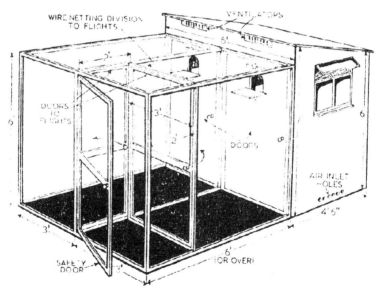

Above: **Ornamental Aviary.**
Bottom: **Simple Aviary Suitable for Parrakeets**

Large Aviary Suitable for Breeding Purposes
Note the shrubs outside and the natural post and perching inside as well as
a climbing plant.

is recommended.

2. The roof should be watertight and easily maintained (a coat of tar and creosote each year should keep it in good order}. Perspex sheets give adequate light, but tend to be cold in winter and hot in summer, although they are acceptable for the covered flight which has wire netting on the outside. Boards and roofing felt are probably the best method for keeping the shed dry, but remember that adequate lighting is still essential within the shed.

3. Windows and entrance holes should be provided for adequate light and exits (which also give some ventilation). Windows should be made so they can be opened, but without draught and properly wire netted so that the birds cannot escape through openings. In addition, shutters or circular outlets fitted to the sides may be used for:

  a) ventilation;

  or

  b) allowing birds to fly through the openings into the outdoor flights (it may be desirable to close these in winter)

4. The floor should be made of wood (above the ground) or concrete. Thick timber, well supported is essential or rats, mice and other vermin will find their way in. Moreover, if not raised above the earth the wood will rot and after a few years will let in damp and cold.

Concrete is obviously the answer, but this tends to be cold so a good covering of clean wood shavings is essential. (renewed when it becomes soiled). Alternatively, a shed with a wooden floor can be placed on concrete or flagstones.

The Bird Room

Aviary and Bird-Room tend to be descriptions of the same thing. However, some people prefer to refer to a bird-room as a specially fitted building, or a room within a building, where all essentials can be kept and the birds can be housed in considerable comfort. Certainly for successful all-the-year-round management well-built insulated accommodation is vital.

An aviary purchased from a garden centre will probably have all the essentials for keeping a few birds, but it will not provide them with all their needs for successful breeding and showing. If space permits, an aviary *and* bird-room may be advisable, thus allowing birds to be kept in comfort at all times as well as providing the means for training for shows. Taken to the ultimate there should also be provision for running water indoors and electricity for light and heat.

INSULATION AND VENTILATION

The aviary or bird-room should be insulated so as to avoid extremes in temperature. If a brick building is used then a wooden frame can be built into the structure with some form of cavity and the inner skin would be plaster board, hard board or one of the many special boards now available. Polystyrene tiles are not suitable because they tend to flake and are a fire hazard. However, some manufacturers have produced special insulating materials for commercial poultry sheds and these could well be worth investigating. Remember though that unless protected with wire netting some parrots will chew all in sight.

Ventilation

The provision of adequate air without excessive draughts should receive attention. This question is also linked with the provision of windows, which may be allowed to open with metal gauze or wire netting to cover the opening.

Small holes drilled in the side of the shed will also provide ventilation as will some form of grille arrangement which will open and close. Ideally the inlet for air should be towards the top of the building. When the air enters it sinks to the ground and, when warmed up, will rise and may be let out at roof level. If the inlet opening is too near the bottom of the building the inrush of air will be too fierce and will cause discomfort.

The aim should be to get the air to circulate so as to remove any foul air or gases, and not to make the aviary too cold. Accordingly, the outside temperature should be considered and in the summer months wire netting covered openings could be beneficial. In winter a different story emerges because the conservation of heat is important, even if there is some loss of ventilation in the bird-room proper (ie, sleeping quarters). Except on very bad days (cold or wet) the birds should always be allowed access to a flight and thereby breathe a plentiful supply of fresh air.

Some breeders never use any heat in a bird-room, whereas others insist that no results are possible without the means of keeping the temperature at not less than around 50° F. Certainly for making an early start with breeding and to make sure that water does not freeze some form of heating is advisable.

In modern times the tendency is to employ tubular heaters which are totally enclosed and use a small amount of electricity. A typical heater is shown opposite; it is usually supplied in convenient lengths of around 1 metre upwards and can be fitted easily and requires no maintenance. Because of its lower power consumption it may be operated without a thermostat simply being turned off when the weather is mild.

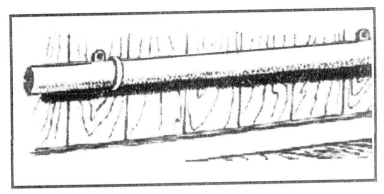

Typical Tubular Heater

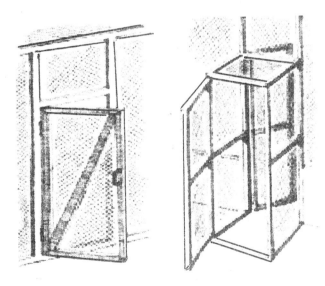

Low Door & Safety Porch which Act
as Safety Devices to Prevent Escape

The position of the aviary also affects heat and light. The author has an aviary at the side of a large lawn with hedges on one side and a wire netting front at the other. Any day when there is sun its rays catch the front of the aviary and give light and warmth. On the other hand, a shed and aviary in a wooded area tends to be extremely suitable in the Summer, but is bitterly cold in Winter. In such circumstances the author has had bantams succumb to the severe; frosts which accumulate in the trees so imagine what can happen to an aviary bird.

This is not to suggest that parrot-like birds are not hardy. They will stand considerable cold and variations in weather once acclimatised, but if early breeding is required with fertile eggs from the first clutch of eggs then you must give them shelter from cold winds, snow and rain.

LIGHTING

Light affects birds and provides the stimulation to lay. Accordingly, the provision of adequate light is essential in two forms:

a) Windows and netted fronts

b) Electric lights controlled by a time switch so that the desired amount of light can be given.

There is no hard and fast rule on the length of period of lighting to give. On poultry breeding and laying there has been considerable research and broadly speaking around 16-17 hours light is regarded as the standard at which to aim. This means the automatic switch is regulated to bring on the light early in the morning to cut off when natural light is adequate and then to switch back on for a further period in the evening.

An alternative is to turn on the light from a switch in the house and then turn if off last thing at night. If this is done a day of around 12 hours is the norm and many breeders have found this acceptable. Certainly if too much light is given there is a danger of stress to the birds. The intensity of light is also important; a small wattage will be adequate, say, 25 watts for an 2.5 x 3 m. house, but use two lights in a long area.

Painting the building inside with a white paint will also affect the light. Lighter paints reflect light better than the darker shades so obviously it is better to use white or some other light colour. Outdoor emulsion or an oil-based paint is advisable.

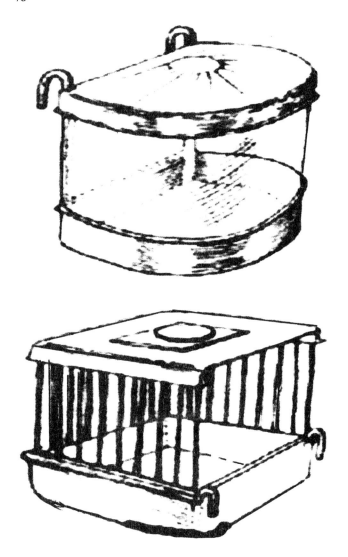

Bird Baths for Smaller Parrakeets
A large tray will be suitable for the larger Parrakeets

PROTECTION FROM DISEASE AND PREDATORS

Birds should be protected from disease and provided common sense rules are followed there should be no problem. Some of the more obvious precautions are as follows :

1. Feed good quality food and watch for mould or bacteria appearing.

2. Clean out food hoppers on a regular basis.

3. Remove sand or sawdust used on the floor at regular intervals. Make sure cobwebs are removed and go round breeding cages with a vacuum cleaner removing all dust -- obviously removing birds before this is done. Give this a thorough clean at least once a year, preferably twice, and make sure every part is cleaned and disinfected. Also clean out cupboards and any place where vermin may lurk.

4. Spray the cages and stock with anti-mite spray and check that the birds are free from parasites. A check should be made at night with torch light to see if red mite exist.

5. Watch out for small access holes gnawed by mice or other creatures (including Parrot-like birds!) and block these. If the invasion persists place bait where mice can get it, but well away from the birds.

6. Keep adequate water in the house and change it regularly. Wash out the utensils in a mild solution of disinfectant (suitable for the purpose) and then rinse thoroughly with clean running water.

7. Have a bird bath so the birds can keep themselves clean.

8. Wash fresh green food stuff in a colander and then remove all surplus. A salad strainer is ideal for this purpose. With insecticides being used the washing is a precaution in case the green food has been sprayed. Where chick weed and other greens are grown in the garden it may be quite safe to feed without washing.

9. The outside flight should have a floor of small pebbles, or gravel, which can be washed down. Alternatively, grass may be sown, although this is not likely to last very long with a number of birds in captivity. Some plant shrubs, but these must be selected carefully.

Concrete floors are a possibility, but these tend to be cold and should be covered with earth or sand. They at least keep out predators. On that subject it is advisable to block the bottom of a flight so that it is predator proof.

Putting wire into the ground and concreting under the bottom cross pieces is advisable or rats, cats, squirrels and other nuisances will gain access.
10. Observe the birds carefully and when illness is apparent, isolate the birds in question and where appropriate use the hospital cage or a separate room which is kept quite warm.

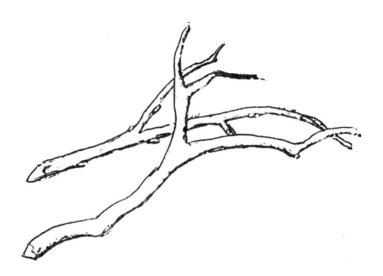

Natural Perches Cut from trees

PERCHES AND RELATED EQUIPMENT

Parrots and Parrakeets are perch users and, therefore, perches must be regarded as an essential part of the equipment of the bird-room and flight. There are a number of places to consider:

1. Cages

Perches are placed from front to back and arranged so that the occupants can jump and fly from one to the other.

2. Birdrooms

Neat uniform perches may be employed, positioned so that some are higher than others thus enabling the birds to fly around. .

3. Flights or Outdoor Aviaries

Natural perches made from the fallen branches of pine trees or fruit trees provide an excellent means of giving all that is necessary with the added advantage of being pleasing in appearance. Branches containing twigs can be nailed into position in the corners or hanging from the ceiling and the birds enjoy moving from one section to another. Perches should be of varying sizes and may be oval or round. The earlier fanciers seemed to prefer the round type whereas today the oval shaped are the first choice for the smaller birds.

The fact remains that the size should be adequate for the bird to exercise its feet and rest. A typical size is 5/8 ths inch (17mm) for small birds, but parrots require at least 1 inch (25mm) and there are some points to watch:

a) Use soft wood rather than hard and/or slippery wood.*

b) Ensure that the perch is firm so that it does not slip around when the bird alights.

c) Consider using a tapered perch which is broad at one end (say 1 inch or around 25mm) and tapers to 1/2 inch (12mm).

d) For outside flights keep the perches away from the wire netting or cats may attack the birds whilst they are perching.

---

*This is a debatable matter; if too soft some Parrakeets will quickly devour the perches, but it is their natural instinct! Fortunately some Parrakeets do very little chewing.

e) In siting perches in an outside flight remember to leave sufficient space for flying. Poor positioning of perches and branches may restrict the area available for flight.

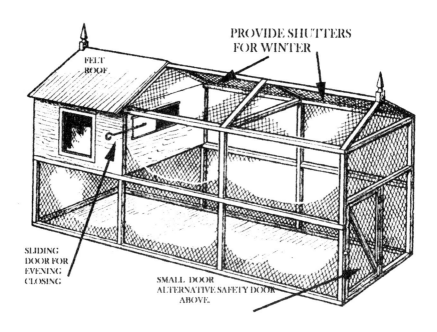

PROVIDE SHUTTERS
FOR WINTER

FELT
ROOF

SLIDING
DOOR FOR
EVENING
CLOSING

SMALL DOOR
ALTERNATIVE SAFETY DOOR
ABOVE.

Basic Aviary

This allows perches to be placed in different positions so the birds can fly from one side (or end) to the other

SAFETY PORCHES

Access to buildings and aviaries without danger of losing birds is an essential consideration when planning accommodation. The most simple way is to have a large shed and then have a "porch" inside which allows easy access. The main compartment is kept separate with an independent door.

The disadvantage with this method is the fact that part of the bird house is wasted although this may be used to store food and equipment in regular use. Shelves can be placed on the walls and tins and boxes kept there. Other possibilities are as follows:

1. Double Door/Low Level Door

A solid door outside and wire netting inside will allow access (with care) but can be hazardous when going in and out. Such an arrangement can be used to keep a bird-room cool in the summer. With a low level (small) door the birds cannot escape as easily as when a tall entrance door is used.

2. External Porches

A porch may be built on to the external door so that easy access is possible. A person entering steps inside and then closes the door before opening the main door to the bird-room without difficulty.

Many fanciers rely on an external aviary as a form of porch, but in this case great care must be taken to ensure that birds do not fly out when the door is opened.

LANDSCAPING AND AESTHETIC REQUIREMENTS

Landscaping is the designing of the aviary and the surrounding areas so that they are pleasing to the eye and more attractive to the birds. Possible additions are as follows:

1. Rustic poles for the outside flight.

2. Climbing shrubs up the side of the flight.

3. A small pond with a fountain.

4. Evergreen shrubs such as laurel and rhododendron outside the bird-room and flight

5. Ornate structures, including brick buildings, tiled roof, elaborate windows and wrought ironwork.

The aesthetic requirements relate to the appearance of the aviary . Looking at a design in a negative way we can suggest that the following features should be avoided :

a) Corrugated sheets which tend to rust and look unsightly (although properly maintained they may be acceptable for the bottom of a flight).

b) Sheds which are knocked together from off-pieces of wood and appear untidy and look amateurish.

If the fancier is to make his own bird-houses then they must be done to an acceptable standard.

c) Aviaries which are not maintained properly so that felt is hanging off the roof and boards are rotting for lack of paint or preservative.

Lean-To Aviary with Flights Attached

Aviary with brick wall which deters predators and gives shelter.

PARROT-LIKE BIRDS
IN AN OUTDOOR AVIARY

Parrot-like birds will do well in garden aviaries, where, contrary to general opinion, they will live quite comfortably all the year round, as regardless of the weather as our common sparrows, or even more so. The birds in an aviary have no anxiety about food, or any trouble in finding or getting at it; and if they have a dry place to roost in, do not seem to feel the cold at all, but will fly around and chatter as freely in the snow as if a summer sun were shining over head.

Nesting out-of-doors

If the aviary is turfed and has shrubs growing in it, the hens will make their nests in the nest boxes provided.

Material for Nests

Parrots and parrot-like birds use bark and chips of wood for nesting. Accordingly, wood shavings would be appropriate. .

Mice

Mice are the great trouble in an outdoor aviary , and they can be kept out of it only with difficulty. The little brutes seem capable of forcing their way through almost the smallest meshed wire that is made; or, if they are baffled in that direction, they will burrow underground, often making quite long tunnels, and will get into the enclosure where least expected. By placing tin or fine wire netting all round the aviary, bent in the shape of the letter L, they are puzzled for a long time; and if all the horizontal part and half of the upright portion of the tin plate are underground, the mice will be baffled in their attempts to gain an entrance for a longer period still. I have, however, known them work their way in through a thick layer of cement, and even through a brick wall.

How to get rid of Mice

Should the aviarist find that nothing will keep the vermin outside his aviary , he will have to poison them in it; but in doing this he will have to be e.xtremely careful that his birds do not pick up any of the poison intended for their enemies. The Warfarin poison is very effective and can be left for long periods provided it remains dry.

Putting in a small cage or enclosed box with entrance hole isolates the poison from the birds. Needless to remark, when all the mice have been killed the small cage should be at once thoroughly cleansed, or better still, burned, which will effectually prevent any accident from an incautious use of it afterwards. Should more mice, after a time, appear upon the scene, they must be served in the same way, for if they are allowed about they will sadly interfere with the nesting birds, and small will indeed be the aviarist's success where the little pests exist in any number.

Cats

Cats are another intolerable nuisance to the aviariest, but can be kept out of the garden by surmounting the high wall with wire-netting, about 1 metre high, and inclined inwards at an angle of about forty-five degrees. No cat will face that, and the birds will be left in peace.

SITE FOR AVIARY

As regards the construction of a garden aviary, it is not my intention to say much for aviaries vary infinitely, according to the taste and purse of the designer and builder; but a few general directions will not be amiss. Always select a wall (or build one, if necessary) for a background or have a strong wooden windbreaker for one wall. Lawn-aviaries open to the air all round are pretty to look at, but unsafe for birds, which are exposed in them to every blast that blows; and as the wind from some quarters is very bitter and searching, it is as well not to subject birds to its influence. The aviary should be erected against a wall that faces either south, south-west, or even south-east; but an aspect due east, or one into which north enters, must be avoided. If no other aspect is available, the fancier had better forego the delight of an outdoor aviary, and keep his birds indoors.

FOOD IN OUTDOOR AVIARY

The feeding of birds out of doors is no different to that recommended for such of these birds as are kept in the house; but more green stuff may be allowed, and almost anything will do (except watercress), with the precaution that no stale vegetable matter be left on the floor of the aviary, which must be kept clean. If the flight part of the aviary is turfed, the birds will want little else in the way of green food, but some rape-seed may be advantageously sown in a border against the wall, and covered with a wire to keep the birds off it, until it is sufficiently grown for their use.

Top of Aviary Showing Glass Roof

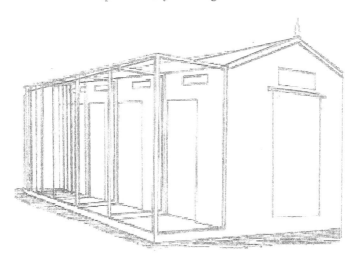

Drawing of Main Bird Room & Separate Aviaries for Breeding

SHRUBS

Unless the aviary is a very large one, and not too many birds are kept in it, there will not be much use in attempting to grow plants, or even trees, within it, for the birds will soon pick them to pieces, not so much to eat as for sheer mischief, or, may be, occupation. The better plan is to introduce plants in pots or small tubs, which can be removed when the plants have been disfigured, and be replaced by others.

I have found ivy, euonymus, and the different kinds of elder (the common, golden, silver, and parsley-leaved) resist their attacks better than anything else. Lilac and laburnum are both poisonous, especially the latter, and must on no account be allowed in an aviary , no matter what birds are kept.

For landscaping many shrubs or climbers may be used and whilst the latter can be very attractive, as well as covering the wire netting, a climber may become very heavy and make the wire sag.

If the aviary is quite large bushes may be planted which give a natural nesting site. However, a concrete floor in the flights does allow the area to be washed down every few months.

SPECIAL STRUCTURE FOR
PARROT-LIKE BIRDS

Parrots and many of the smaller parrot-like birds do chew wood and nibble the aviary until it disintegrates. This applies to perches, nest boxes, framework of the aviary and the house in which they live. Accordingly, even if birds which are inclined to be non-destructive, such as Kakarikis, it is better to anticipate problems and use wood of a thickness suitable for all types of parrakeets. Alternatively, protect the inside with ply-board or netting.

Some breeders advocate the use of steel uprights and cross pieces to prevent damage and for the large parrots these are advised. They suffer from being rather ugly and not easily fitting into a garden, whereas wooden structures can be made to look quite natural and, in any case, Parrakeets do not give really serious problems.

OPPOSITE
Aviary with Bushes Growing
For some Parrakeets this may not be acceptable because the birds should have plenty of flying room.

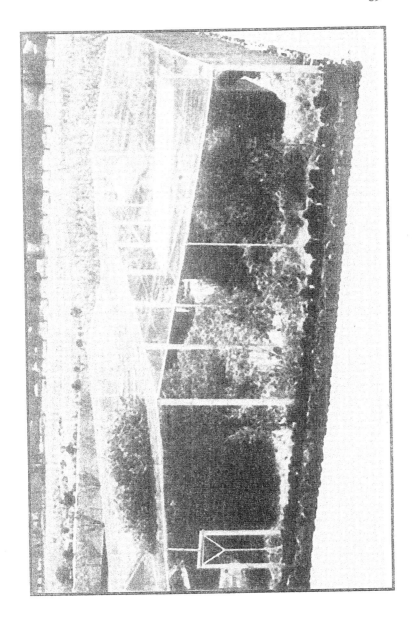

WOODEN STRUCTURES

Normal sheds and aviaries purchased from bird/garden centres are not usually suitable for parrot-like birds unless ordered specially or modified. Quite thick boards would be necessary -- 1 inch thick (25mm) and preferably tongue and grooved so there is nothing the birds can grasp and chew. For large parrots all wooden structures should be covered with wire netting. There is no need for this action when dealing with parrakeets.

Leaving the posts and cross pieces outside the wire is also an alternative method. Provided the birds cannot get at the wood then it cannot be destroyed.

RANGE OF FLIGHTS

Parrakeets may be housed in small aviaries, located side-by-side, thus allowing many breeding pairs to be kept. A corridor may be placed down the middle of the back of the unit thus allowing access to the sleeping q uarters. Alternatively, this may be at the end of each pen.

WELFARE AND HYGIENE

An aviary with a grass surface or bare earth has some advantages, but very quickly becomes "stale" and disease-ridden.

The alternative is to have stone chips, pebbles or concrete which enables a site to be a permanent home for the birds. Sometimes bird keepers suggest moving the aviary/flight around a lawn or paddock and this certainly keeps the ground fresh. It can be very inconvenient and cumbersome except for very small structures. However, it does work wonderfully when it can be applied.

A method used by the author is the regular adding of leaves, leaf mould, grass clippings, weeds and other garden bi-products to the floor of the aviary. This keeps the ground fresh, provides items of interest to the birds and is a method of disposing of leaves, etc. without difficulty.

Moreover a carpet of leaves resembles the conditions birds find in the wild and therefore is quite acceptable to the birds. However, as already stressed, make sure that old greens and other materials which become mouldy, are not left to accumulate or the birds may catch some infection. Clean out at least once per week.

SIZE OF AVIARY

For those with limited space a 2 m. x 1 m. flight with sheltered roost is quite adequate for even a large species. The smaller Parrakeets can manage with half that size. Remember if flights are too large the Parrakeets will fly around rather wildly and lose their tameness. At breeding time the concentration should be on keeping the birds steady with minimum interference so a small flight is advisable.

Aviary Flight in Corner Site

Situated between two buildings it provides excellent shelter and is economical to build.

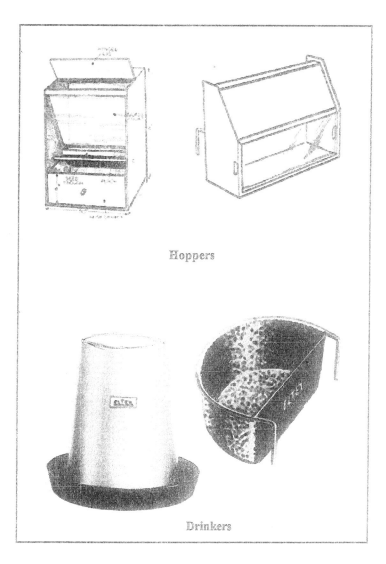

Hoppers

Drinkers

Variety of Food & Water Utensils

CHAPTER 6
FEEDING

HOW OFTEN?

Food and water are absolutely vital constituents in the life and well being of all birds. Get the diet right and much else will be satisfactory. There are different points of view on how often birds should be fed and what they should be given. Moreover, each *Genus* and related species does have a type of food most suitable for its requirements, as near as possible to its natural food.

The *form* in which the food is taken should also be considered. For example, large parrakeets with their powerful beaks will eat apples, oranges, grape fruits, carrots and other suitable fruit or vegetables without having to be cut. Simply spiking on a nail is adequate. When dealing with Grass Parrakeets (Turquoisines, and Rosellas etc.) fruit should be sliced or they are unlikely to touch it. Pelleted food has been quite successful with some breeders, but others cannot persuade their birds to take pellets. My experience has been that sunflower seed and other seeds, plus greens have been the main stay, with soaked bread in hot weather, but pellets were very unpopular.

DAILY FEEDING

The *pros and cons* of daily feeding (twice per day) are as follows:

Advantages

1. Birds learn to associate humans with food and look forward to receiving the due meal. This should lead to a closer relationship between captive and bird keeper. The birds can become quite tame.
It will be noted that hand reared parrots are much more expressive than aviary bred birds which are on the wild side. The tame birds learn to talk more easily.

2. Fair shares should be possible for all and any that appear to be missing out can be given a supplementary feed.

SPECIAL NOTE In practice, when the birds are kept quite hungry, the weaker birds may starve so great care must be taken to see that none is neglected.

3. Over feeding is avoided so the birds are fitter and more inclined to search for food in between meals.

4. Being hungry means that a varied and balanced diet will be taken quite readily.

5. Waste is minimised because the amount the birds eat quickly; say, in 20 minutes, can be calculated.

The early morning meal would be given before 9.00 a.m. and the later one around 4.00 p.m, depending on weather and daylight available. The food is scattered where appropriate; e.g., on a bench or on the floor for ground feeding birds.

Often a combination of the two methods would be appropriate. Remember, also, they like to eat sprouting seeds so a small amount of surplus should be allowed to scatter.

Possible disadvantages of daily feeding are as follows:

1. With a hobby, fanciers do not always have the time to feed each day so a container of food is left which is sufficient for a few days.

2. Parrot-like birds prefer to eat early morning and late evening, but also take additional food during the day. Often they are reluctant to take food when being watched.

3. When some birds are bullied they will hang back and not be fed, but if a supply of seed is available they will take it when others are not feeding.

In practice, with the hobbyist, a compromise is necessary. The basic seeds are left in a dish or dishes and extras are fed once a day. Thus apples and fruit are placed on spikes each day and titbits are given as required; e.g. millet sprays, soaked bread, greens.

WHAT TO FEED

Pet shops sell Parrakeet mixture this is usually more suitable for the smaller species such as Grass Parrakeets.   Parrot mixture contains more variety, but some may be wasted.   This would include sunflower seeds, peanuts, maize and various items such as peas and small peppers.

   If the birds will take canary seed -- usually recommended, but not always taken -- this can be put in a separate dish. It is advisable to have separate dishes for doubtful items,   and then the consumption can be measured. Any new foods can be tested in this way.

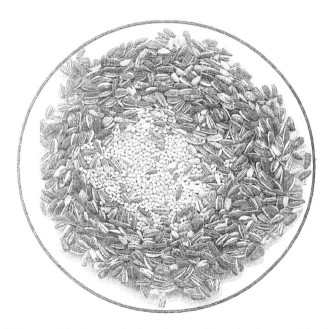

Mixture of Sunflower Seed on the outside and other seeds in the middle

Possible Foods

1. Sunflower, maize, oats, wheat, peanuts, peas
2. Bread-soaked in milk or water or just plain
3. Apples, pears and other fruit
4. Green stuff such as chickweed and vegetable -- carrots, turnips etc.

Some fanciers also try dog food (ground biscuit), poultry crumbs, and other pet foods. In practice, sunflower seed and fruit, especially apples, appear to be the main foodstuffs with the occasional millet spray and bunches of chickweed. However, variety is vital and the principles of feeding are explained in the next section.

Sprouting seeds are also given, especially when young are being reared . This may be done by using sprouting bowls or simply by throwing seeds on the earth floor and allowing them to germinate naturally; in a dry period spray them with water. However, take care not to place them where they can be fouled by birds' droppings.

How Much Food ?

Attempts are sometimes made to specify how much food should be given to a species. This is very difficult because individual birds have preferences and may eat more of one type of food than another, leaving some seeds uneaten. Unfortunately, parrot-like birds are extremely wasteful.

Many breeders have found that they eat a considerable amount of sunflower seed and fruit but little else. Yet, desirably, they should have roughage in the form of wholemeal bread. Accordingly, variety is essential, but minimising waste is also necessary. Piles of unwanted food leads to trouble and should be avoided be clearing away any food left and learn to give the correct portions.

If we assume as a rough guide that an adult will eat , say, 50 grammes each day about 20 grammes will be in sunflower seed. The balance will be sprouted seeds (including oats or wheat) -- say 10 grammes, peas, and maize (say 5 grammes) and the balance in wholemeal bread (5.8 grammes) and the remainder in titbits and various small seeds and other desirable foods. This is only a rough guide. Birds may be given this amount, but are often quite wasteful so stale food must be removed and the more accurate amount estimated.

Grit Essential

The provision of grit and small flints, and cuttlefish bone as well as water, will be vital requirements in the feeding programme. Vitamin supplements should also be considered, but do not get carried away with this idea because a varied and ample diet should cover all essentials.

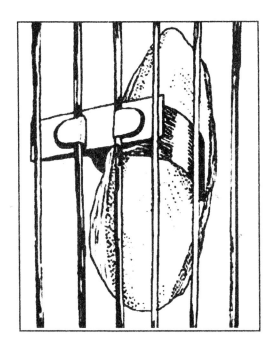

Cuttle Fish Bone in Holder
An alternative holder is a Bulldog Clip
Fine grit may also be provided.

VARIETY ESSENTIAL

As for all other parrot-like birds a variety of foods should be given. An understanding of food values is essential and as a background study some relevant notes are now given. Food science has advanced a great deal and the requirements of a balanced diet have been studied and Parrot pellets can be obtained, but not all parrots will eat them so a practical approach is essential. Balanced, mixed feeding, provides enjoyment and avoids boredom.

A fancier desires to have healthy birds and this means the correct environment and adequate food which usually means a balanced diet.

The essential components are as follows:
1. Proteins
2. Carbohydrates (starches)
3. Fats
4. Water

Food technology is now also able to specify the mineral content of food, but remembering a *balanced diet* is essential, is good enough for everyday purposes. For this to be calculated, it is necessary that the fancier should have some knowledge of the food content of the various seeds and other foods, following which he will then be able to provide the *essential balance*.

Opposite is a table of seeds and other foods which sets out the constituents.

BASIC CONSTITUENTS

As noted, there are three basic constituents necessary in the diet of all living creatures; namely, **proteins, carbohydrates** and fat. These three elements must be contained in any given diet, and what is more important, they must be balanced against each other if all of the dietary requirementsof the birds are to be met.

Protein

It is frequently, and perhaps correctly, argued that protein is the most essential constituent in the diet of any type of bird life. Protein is the substance which builds the muscles and which will quite literally put the meat on the bones. It also gives energy.

Canary Seed	15.0	14.0	52.0	5.50	86.50
Rape Seed	7.0	22.0	20.0	40.0	89
Maw Seed	9.0	19.0	18.0	45.0	91
Millet Seed	14.0	15.0	57.0	4.0	93
Linseed	9.0	23.0	23.0	24.0	79
Hemp Seed	11.0	16.0	25.0	30.0	83
Niger Seed	12.0	21.0	22.0	40.0	95
Lettuce	95.0	1.0	2.0	0.2	99.2
Dandelion	84.0	2.4	10.6	1.0	98
Carrot	87.0	1.2	9.6	0.1	97.9
Apple	83.0	0.5	15.0	Nil	98.5
Egg Yolk	47.0	15.0	Nil	33.0	95
Egg White	87.0	10.0	Nil	0.25	97.25
Sunflower Seed	6.0	24.0	21.0	49.0	100

Food Values of Different Foods

Carbohydrates

Another essential part of the diet is the carbohydrate content. This is the dietary element which gives energy and which is used up rapidly by the body processes, especially when exercise is being taken, rather in the same way as coal is consumed in a fire.

Fat (Oils) within Food

Fats are another important part of the diet. These elements supplement the carbohydrates and also generate body heat. However, excessive amounts can be harmful and must be controlled, especially when it is noted that some favourite seeds are very high in oil content.

From this information, it can clearly be seen that the emphasis on a *balanced diet* cannot be stressed too strongly. What, for example, is the point in giving a diet which is overloaded with protein, if the carbohydrates are insufficient to burn up the excess proteins? In such a case, the result would be obesity in the stock rather than a balanced type of bird. Pieces of fat are not recommended. Remember that *variety* keeps birds interested and active, thus avoiding bad habits such as feather pecking.

SPECIAL NOTES ON FOOD VALUES

1. Growing feathers, beaks, and toenails requires an extra amount of protein and, therefore, young birds should be given a special diet containing a high level of protein.

2. Amino Acids are essential for growth and, therefore, must be present in the diet. A variety of seeds is essential for the bird to achieve the level of amino acids it requires.

3. Vitamins. These are essential to the well being of seed eaters. They are:

a) Vitamin A -- fish liver oil is the best source; but greens and carrots are also essential and are taken readily. A deficiency will result in poor breeding results, constant colds (breathing difficulties, watery eyes and thick mucous around the nostrils).
Cod-liver oil should be mixed daily with the seed and the wild greens listed later. In addition, lettuce, spinach, kale and other fresh greens should be given. Bleached vegetables should not be given and cabbage or brussels sprouts do not give a high level of vitamin A.

b) Vitamin D -- Lack of vitamin D results in leg, joint, beak and other bone growth problems (rickets). Adding cod liver oil and feeding calcium in some form will help to combat the deficiency, but sunshine is the essential requirement. The ultra violet rays from the sun are vital and special lamps can provide rays, but may damage the eyes of the birds, due to being too strong. Sunshine through clear glass is not helpful because the ultra violet rays may not pass through.

c) Vitamin E -- This vitamin provides the necessary component for reproduction. Its main source is sprouting seeds such as wheat and certain leaf plants such as lettuce; watercress and spinach. Egg yolk is also a prime source. However, wheat germ oil should be mixed separately from cod-liver oil, although the two can be used on seed provided they are mixed separately.

d) Water-soluble Vitamins -- Many vitamins may be purchased in the form of a soluble solution such as *Abidec* and many fanciers find that this method is adequate. However, greenstuff and egg food are still vital and should not be omitted.

IMPORTANCE OF FRESH SEED

If poor quality, dirty or contaminated seed is used the birds will starve or will suffer from diseases of one sort or another. A seed is made up of a number of parts:

     a) **Shell**

     b) **Embryo (proteins and vitamins, etc.)**

     c) **Endosperm (starches)**

SPECIAL NOTE

Each seed is a living organism which should be capable of germinating; if not, then it should not be fed to birds. The first part to deteriorate is usually the germ part (the embryo) which contains the proteins and, without which, a bird will suffer various ill effects, such as running eyes -- eventually it will starve.

Problems with seeds which are deteriorating are as follows:

     a) **Infested with mould and fungi.**

     b) **Contaminated with chemicals or oil due to faulty**

     storage.

     c) **Mixed with dust and/or other undesirable elements,**

     including mite or weevils.

     d) **Smelling musty or rancid.**

     e) **Too old or kept in warm humid conditions. A cool well**

     ventilated atmosphere is desirable.

If dusty or smells rancid, then it should not be used in any form.

SPROUTING SEEDS

Many bird fanciers believe wholeheartedly that sprouted seed should be integral part of the diet of cage birds. It is agreed that sprouting reduces the starch and increases the protein and, in addition, makes the seed more easily digested. They spend hours each month preparing and feeding the sprouted seeds and certainly many birds seem to relish the processed food.

In recent times, doubt has been cast on the wisdom of using sprouted seed and whilst there is not conclusive proof that the practice is harmful the following facts should be considered:

1. Soaking brings about a chemical reaction in the seed and changes the starch to sugar. This in itself is not harmful but if the seeds are left in the water, without adequate exposure to the air, they begin to deteroriate. In fact, if left longer than 24 hours the seed will begin to die. An experiment carried out in the USA found that birds fed with seeds soaked for 48 hours would not lay.

2. Many of the proteins may be released into the water.

3. From observations made it would appear that soaked seeds do not digest properly. Soaking appears to give them some kind of protection against the digestive juices; in fact, nestlings fed by their parents will usually pass the soaked seeds through their system without any change in composition.

SPECIAL NOTE: Most of the arguments are against badly soaked seeds so any to be soaked should be germinated on a stainless steel or plastic dish and kept damp (not soaked) by means of gauze which rests in water. Absolute cleanliness is essential to avoid contamination.

CONDITIONS REQUIRING DIFFERENT
OR SUPPLEMENTED FOOD

When feeding birds it is essential to consider the following:

1. Normal feeding for healthy stock.

2. Feeding for breeding.

3. Food for moulting.

4. Supplements or special food for periods of stress, e.g. when moulting or when sick.

NORMAL FEEDING

The comments made earlier apply to this situation. A balanced diet is essential and fed regularly so that the birds have ample food without this standing around too long.

When dealing with domesticated birds, such as poultry, we can state precisely what quantity is necessary for growing, laying and so on. With poultry, around , say, 6 oz. per laying hen will be fed (depends on breed). This is a precise measure. However, with cage birds the amount eaten is not proportionate to the relative weight of a fowl and, say, canaries or parrots. Some food they will peck out of the hopper, others they will leave, and there is no standardisation as for poultry.

A parrot prefers different food from a budgerigars, although they belong to the same family. Each bird fancier must find out the likes and dislikes of his birds and feed accordingly.

FOOD FOR MOULTING

A great deal is written about the problems of the moult and yet in the correct environment there is generally no problem. The fact remains that the growing of feathers requires *extra* protein and vitamins. Soft food is usually recommended and tonic seeds (rich in oil) should also be given.

The annual shedding of feathers takes place as the weather changes and becomes colder. In the UK this occurs around the middle of September and goes on for a few weeks; it may occur earlier or later, but usually an attempt is made to have birds back in condition for the November shows.

Some fanciers have special cages for moulting birds, whereas others simply separate the cocks. When birds are transferred they should be taken in pairs or threes so they are placed in their new abode together, thus avoiding conflict when single birds are placed in a cage at different times. At the early stages of the moulting period feed a plain diet and water until feathers begin to fall. A bird is through the moult when the new head feathers are fully grown.

During the moult there should be adequate ventilation and moderate exercise. A plentiful supply of the greenstuff is essential and sweet apples are recommended at the rate of one per day per bird. If they do not eat them try an alternative fruit. Bananas are popular with some Parrakeets, but not others and they certainly lose their freshness quickly so limited amounts of chopped bananas should be given.

Additional Notes

For the novice additional notes are now added, compiled by a well known bird keeper:

1. Green Food

Some breeders advocate a liberal supply of green food for breeding birds, while others look upon it as little short of a deadly poison; and here it may be remarked that both sides are right to a certain extent, for much depends upon the kind and quality of the green stuff supplied to the birds.

Nature provides a valuable part of the supplementary food required by Parrakeets. Greenstuff is a vital part of the diet and wild seeds help to provide oil and other essentials for beautiful plumage.

The main green foods are as follows:

(a) Chickweed which is very popular and nutritious (although some fanciers do not like to feed chick weed)

(b) Dandelion which provides many essentials such as calcium, iron and magnesium

(c) Mustard seed   (d) Plantain

(e) Shepherd's purse (f) Teazle (g) Dock

Lettuce is a good substitute, but wilts quickly so should be kept in the cold box in a refrigerator and given daily, just sufficient for the day.

A little should be given once a day and should be varied to stimulate the appetite. Important   wild seeds are those taken from dock,   maw, persicaria, gold of pleasure and plantain. PLANTS FROM THE GARDEN SHOULD BE WASHED, because fertilisers may be on them; also disease may be on tainted plants.

2. Basic Foods

Food stuffs of seeds of various types supplemented with vitamins, oils and minerals. In addition, wild plants and fruit should be given on a regular basis, thus keeping the birds in peak condition.

A balanced diet is essential and this should be formulated on the basis of whether dealing with birds for breeding or when moulting, or for normal feeding. Birds will then usually acquit themselves of their parental duties.

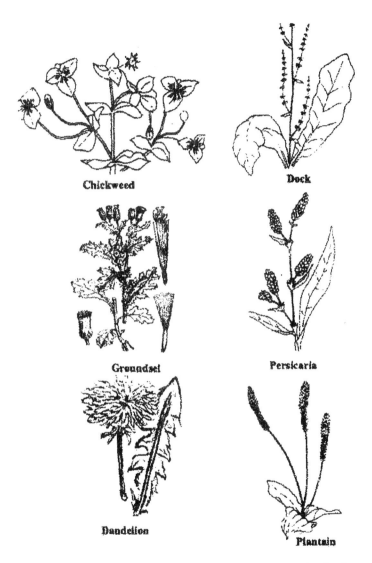

Chickweed

Dock

Groundsel

Persicaria

Dandelion

Plantain

Various Grenstuff which should be fed on a regular basis.
Even short grass and clover is appreciated.

But sometimes they will not, and it is only fair to say that there are birds that no plan or system of feeding will induce to attend to their offspring for more than a few days, or a week or two at the outside.

SOAKED SEEDS

Whether to give soaked seed is arguable and the birds do not always take to it so a trial should be carried out. The best quality seed is put to soak in cold fresh water. When taken from the vessel in which it has been soaked, the seed should be wiped dry with a clean towel or other cloth, or it should be strained thoroughly as part of the process. If this precaution is neglected, the seed will stick together in a lump, will be difficult for the birds to get at, and will, moreover, be liable to turn sour.

The seed must be prepared from day to day and if put to soak in the morning, when the birds are being attended to, will be ready by the same hour on the following day. Regularity in this respect reduces the "trouble" to a minimum. However, those with limited time may prefer to rely on mixed seed and other varables, such as greenstuff from the garden or fields.

SEED-HOPPERS

Several kinds of seed-hoppers have been invented, with the object of guarding against waste. Many birds make a practice of scattering their seed- - in search, no doubt, of something of which they are in want or like and these hoppers are useful in their way, but as much care is necessary to keep the contents clean and free from dust in their case as in that of the ordinary kind. The type of dish preferred by the author is a large open and shallow type which allows maximum exposure of seeds.

WATER

An important point, and one that is too often overlooked is to keep the drinking water pure and clean, for birds, especially when bread or eggs are fed, are apt to quickly spoil it by dipping their beaks into the fountain or cup while particles of food are still adhering to their mandibles.

It will be as well, particularly in hot weather, to change the water and cleanse the vessel that holds it several times a day, for the particles of egg and other food quickly decompose, and are apt to give rise to trouble --some diarrhoea in both old and young. Sterilize the container with bleach or disinfectant every month or so, but be sure to rinse with cold water in a thorough way, so the birds suffer no ill effects.

CALCIUM

Calcium is essential for the development of egg shells and as part of diet. In addition, *insoluble grit* must be provided for digesting the food; e.g, flint at the appropriate size.

The mixture to be given should include:

1. **Cuttle-fish bone**
2. **Washed river sand**
3. **Oyster shell**
4. **Charcoal finely ground**

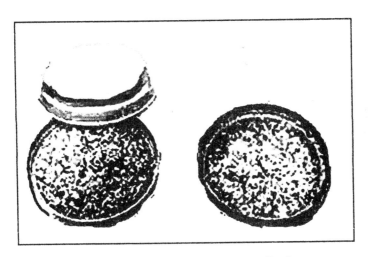

Small Plastic Containers & Soaking Seeds

GETTING THE CORRECT BALANCE

As noted above, the typical foods contain different proportions of protein, carbohydrates and fat. Getting the correct balance is important but also difficult.

Like humans, birds have periods when they like one form of food rather than another. The weather, time of year, whether breeding or moulting all make a difference. The author finds that citrus fruits, such as grapefruits are eaten only in the summer months.

In addition, there is habit -- what foods have been fed in the past, especially in the early stages of development. When new birds are acquired there is always difficulty in getting the mixture correct and, indeed, it is advisable to ask the previous owner for details of the diet.

The vital foods also include various fruits, greens and soft food as described earlier .

BASIC RULES – SUMMARY

1. FEED ON A REGULAR BASIS AND CLEAR HUSKS AWAY EVERY FEW DAYS.
Some bird keepers maintain a small collection of other birds such as doves, quail ,or bantams, which clear away discarded food. These are ground foragers. Obviously a large enough aviary will be essential and *cover* should be provided for the foragers. Quail may suffer in bad weather and for this reason the author prefers a hardy bantam, but not those with feathered legs.

2. PROVIDE AN ADEQUATE AND VARIED DIET:
   (a) Mixed seeds and nuts
   (b) Fruit; e.g. Pears, grapes and apples, bananas, blackberries and dates
   (c) Soft food such as stale bread -- not mouldy, soaked and then the liquid pressed out to make it crumbly (not doughy) or egg food (hard boiled egg sliced and mixed with bread crumbs)
   (d) Green foods such as:

   (i) lettuce, spinach and garden peas

   (ii) wild plants and seeds there from, including chick-

   weed, dock, persicaria and plantain

Banana, Apple and Satsuma Orange
These will need cutting up for the Parrakeets although apples may be
spiked for the larger species.

e) Root vegetables; eg, carrots
(f) Soaked seeds and also sprouting seeds

Do not leave food around too long and feed fresh fruit which is not too ripe. Bananas which have gone to pulp or are blackened are frequently seen in aviaries and are unattractive to most birds.

3. PROVIDE OTHER ESSENTIALS SUCH AS:
   (a) Grit, cuttlefish bone, etc.
   (b) Water
   (c) Vitamins

4. USE SUITABLE FOOD AND WATER UTENSILS SO FOOD IS NOT WASTED.

SEED MIXTURES
As a rough guide it is usual to divide mixtures as follows:

1. Parrots and Parrakeets
(Macaws, Amazons, Cockatoos, African Greys, Ring Necks, etc)
Give a mixture consisting of large nutritious foods such as sunflower seeds, nuts, maize, hemp, canary seed, millet, wheat and niger. Opinions differ on the proportions. Sunflower seeds should form a substantial part. One well known breeder suggests 65% , whereas another believes that 40% is about right, with the balance being made up of canary seed and other food.

Example: Medium Parrot/Large Parrakeet

Canary	30
Millet	5
Hemp	5
Sunflower	50
Oats	5
Peanuts	5
	100%

This mixture is supplied or can be mixed for the larger Parrots, but may also be used occasionally for all Parrakeets who like a change of diet and will pick out the seeds, etc. that they like. It is essential to also provide extras on a daily basis to augment this basic diet which is available at all times.

Egg Sections and Toasted Wholemeal Bread
Egg may be sliced or may be purchased ready mixed in a packet. The left over toast from breakfast can be fed as it is or soaked in milk and then squeezed to make it fairly friable.

2. Parrakeets and Smaller Parrots
(eg, Parrakeets, Lovebirds, Kakarikis, Cockatiels)

A similar mixture to the above, but with more of the smaller seeds. The smaller birds should not be given too much sunflower seed or hemp.

Canary	50
Millet	20
Peanuts	10
Sunflower	10
Safflower	10
	100%

5. PROVIDE A BATH SO THAT BIRDS
CAN SPLASH AROUND AND BATHE THEMSELVES.

A large shallow container is ideal about 22 cm deep and 60cm in diameter, which can be hosed out each day.

HYGIENE IN THE AVIARY

All food should be clean and wholesome. Fruit such as apples should be placed on spikes; eg, nails, so they cannot roll around the aviary.

Greenstuffs should be rinsed to remove possible eggs of worms or other parasites and also to eliminate any chemicals where the plants may have been sprayed. Badly frosted greens should not be fed.

EXERCISE AND HEALTH

Flying from one part of the aviary to another should be encouraged; exercise is vital for fitness and breeding. Giving adequate perches of a wide variety should be the aim. Parrakeets spend their natural lives in trees and gnaw the branches or feed on the ground. Try to simulate these conditions so they live happily.

Put the food in different places so that they have to fly around to reach the different titbits whether apple, chickweed, celery, carrots, or seeds. They are not battery hens so variety is essential. Often you will not see them feeding so watch to see what is taken. Replenish on a daily basis and remove any rejected food, such as over-ripe fruit.

Replacing food, placing fruit on spikes, replacing millet sprays (how they gobble through these !!) and other daily titbits, all help to stimulate interest at a high level so the birds do not become mopey. Remember, these birds use up energy at a frantic rate and this must be allowed for with the feeding.

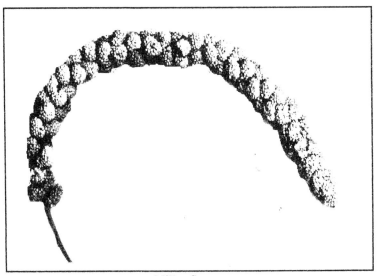

Millet Spray

This is relished by all types of Parrakeets and should be given once per day. Watch out for good quality sprays. Those that are very narrow or obviously old and dusty should not be purchased.

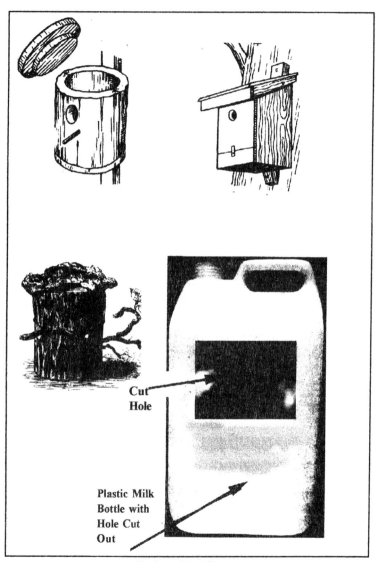

Cut
Hole

Plastic Milk
Bottle with
Hole Cut
Out

Various Nest Boxes

7

BREEDING

BREEDING CATEGORIES

Aviary birds may be classified on the basis of how they fare in the breeding season. Some are quite difficult and, indeed, are very rarely bred in captivity; others are quite easy to reproduce and may just be left to get on with it.

A possible classification might be as possible:

Category

A Easy to breed with no special problems; e.g. Budgerigars, Cockatiels and Kakarikis.

B Fairly straight forward but sometimes presents difficulties, especially when attempting to produce mutations; e.g. Ring-Necks such as the Lutinos, but especially Blues, Greys, and Albinos.

C Difficult to breed, often taking many years of patient endeavour to achieve success; e.g. some of the larger Parrots.

D Very difficult to breed and sometimes no record of any breeding at all; e.g. larger, rare Parrots, although breeding techniques continue to be improved.

PAIRING UP

A cock and a hen should be placed together in an aviary a few months before breeding is expected. In Britain this would be around November, with a view to pairing up taking place by March.

If a number of Parrakeets are kept together in a communal aviary they may pair up before full maturity and, if so, they should be kept together in the separate aviary when breeding is to commence.

When an extremely large aviary is available, with a plentiful supply of nest boxes, breeding may be possible from a number of pairs. Clearly though, there must be a watchfulness. Any problems and any serious fighting, including toe biting (which could result in amputation) must call for swift action. Any birds which show excessive aggression should be separated from the family community .Evidence of pairing up can be seen from the behaviour of the birds. They will be seen together as a pair living in harmony, whereas those that have not found a mate will tend to be aggressive, snapping at any bird which comes within striking distance.

MATING DISPLAY

Mating displays differ according to the species, but which ever way is used the aim is for the cock to attract the hen, often feeding her, and making a fussuntil copulation takes place.

NEST BOXES

Different types of nest boxes will be acceptable but there is a preference for the Grandfather clock type for many Parrakeets ; i.e. an upright type with a hole in the upper part for entry and exit.

Alternatively, a hollowed out log may be used, but may not be easily obtainable. Measurements recommended are 1 x 1 ft. square (30 x 30 cm) and 2 ft deep (60 cm) , but some prefer larger boxes.

The entrance hole should be about 4 inches (10cm) in diameter or a little smaller. A strip of wire netting or twilweld should be placed inside to facilitate entry and exit.

Many breeders have suggested that better results can be obtained by placing the nest boxes in the aviary rather than the entirely covered shelter , but much depends on the level of privacy and environment.

Nesting Material

Opinions differ on the best nest lining but some form of natural material is advised. This may be shavings, leaves, peat, coarse sawdust or decayed wood. It should be placed to a good depth, thus helping to insulate the bottom of the nest box.

Banjo Nest Box

Some fanciers in the past have suggested that a long tunnel should be affixed to the entrance hole of the nest box (then called a "banjo" nest box). With some birds it is believed that the long entrance offers more privacy than the conventional form. Certainly, if it does give a better feeling of security it should be used. However, there are many possibilities and nests made of plastic containers have been accepted without serious problems.

POSITIONING OF NEST BOXES

Most boxes should hang in secluded positions, sheltered from the direct rays of the sun. At the same time they should be accessible for inspection, especially when chicks are in the nest box. They should also be checked to ensure that feeding is taking place.

THE EGGS

In captivity, many Parrakeets usually lay one clutch of eggs and (hopefully) raise one brood of chicks. It is suggested that twice a year is a distinct possibility in the wild, but no doubt the climate influences this matter. Certainly, in Britain, once a year is regarded as the norm. Others lay two batches of eggs and sometimes three, but a pair of birds should not be expected to breed too many chicks in a year.

The number of eggs varies. Usually around four to six eggs are laid. They may differ slightly in size from one sub-species to another.

BREEDING PROBLEMS

Failures in breeding are many and varied and new findings arise quite regularly. Sadly nothing is more frustrating than constant negative results such as:

1. **Non-pairing**   2. **Clear eggs**
3. **Egg binding**   4. **Broken eggs**
5. **Unreliable mothers**
    (a) Unsteady on the nest;
    (b) Not feeding chicks when hatched, sometimes killing them.
6. **Inadequate nesting facilities**

FAILURE TO PAIR-UP

The failure of birds to pair-up is caused by many factors. It is important to check on:

(a) Are male and female being paired?
Sexing can be difficult with some species. Usually the male is heavier in build or has some distinctive feature.

(b) Do the birds get on with each other?
Incompatibility is often present with some Parrakeets (eg, Ring Necks). The females tend to be aggressive and may turn on the male with little or no provocation.
Sometimes one bird is afraid of the other; conversely he or she may have no interest in the mating process.

(c) Unsuitable accommodation or too many distractions.
May be too noisy or there may be other birds in the aviary. Generally speaking Parrakeets should be housed in pairs so that no conflict is possible.

Ideally the birds should "mate up" before puberty. Those birds which are quite incompatible can then be separated.

CLEAR EGGS

The clear eggs after a period of incubation, say, 7 days is a indication that copulation is not taking place in a satisfactory manner. This may be due to an immature male or he may be impotent.

Often it is a combination of factors such as unsuitable housing and food. If birds are allowed to nest too early it may be found that the male is out of condition so the eggs are clear .

When birds nest quite early (February or March) there is always a danger of clear eggs and some breeders recommend not inserting nest boxes until March, so the danger of very early chicks is avoided. It may be more sensible to have an aviary which is well sheltered so that adverse weather conditions are kept away from the birds.

EGG BINDING

An aviary which gives adequate exercise is the most probable cure to egg binding. If it does occur, then the application of olive oil or confinement in a hospital cage may be the answer, but with good feeding practices and adequate exercise there should be no problem.

A common problem is for a hen to have difficulty in laying an egg, which is passing down the oviduct. She will be seen to be out of sorts with ruffled feathers and looking miserable.

Egg binding may be caused by one or more of a number of factors:

> **1. Soft-shelled eggs due to inadequate or unsuitable calcium grit**
>
> **2. Hen too fat and out of condition**
>
> **3. Incorrect diet**
>
> **4. Over heating in the bird-room and nest box**
>
> **5. Constipation causing a partial blockage of the oviduct by exerting pressure**
>
> **6. Old hen who is not strong enough to lay the egg**
>
> **7. Egg too large to be expelled**

Parrakeets can be very difficult with egg binding so prompt attention is essential.

Possible Solutions

Once egg binding has occurred there are many possibilities:

> **a) Do nothing initially, but place the hen into a hospital cage at a temperature of around 75⁰F (25°C) and, provided not too serious, the egg will be laid by the next morning.**
>
> **b) Oil the vent by using a fine brush (castor or olive oil). This may be followed by steaming the vent over hot water (not too hot) placed in a jar or jug with muslin over the top. After five minutes the egg should appear.**

c) Apply the "expression method" of expelling the egg.
This method was advocated by "old time" bird fanciers and is not to be recommended to the amateur fancier who will probably break the egg.

EXPRESSION METHOD

Briefly, the Expression Method, is as follows:

Put bird on its back in left hand, head towards right hand; finger and thumb placed on sides of egg near vent and drawn backwards with gentle pressure on the egg to be sure of pushing aside the intestines and oviduct which lie partially over its surface. When sufficiently drawn back the finger and thumb holding egg between are gently, slowly and firmly pushed forwards towards the vent and the ease with which the egg is expressed into the palm of the hand is magical. I do not think it causes more pain than usual; it is certainly quicker and therefore must relieve the bird of hours of suffering, and as far as I know it is free from any ill effects as it simply imitates nature and supplies the defective expulsive efforts.

Great care and gentleness are required, and a delicate touch -- a very great asset in the accomplishment of the manoeuvre. On no account should the egg be pinched between the finger and thumb, or it will be broken and is then more difficult to get away. Personally, I have done it, i.e., broken it, and got it away successfully, and on the rare occasions that I had an accident, once only, as far as I can remember, it was due to my not taking sufficient time and care in the correct placing of the finger and thumb. Only sufficient pressure should be made to prevent the egg going backwards between the finger and thumb, and the whole arrangement of the egg and finger and thumb should be pushed forwards -- towards the vent.

If the first attempt fails to extrude the egg, it will have at least partially dilated the oviduct end, and a series of gentle pressures forward with re-adjustments of thumb and finger will push the egg down until its greatest diameter has passed the resistance in front, and the manipulation will succeed. The fancier who has a very heavy hand and not a delicate sense of touch would be wise to ask a fellow fancier who is better in these respects to attempt it for him. I think it would be justifiable, if the usually suggested means failed, for otherwise the bird is likely to die.

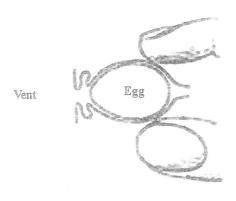

Expression Method of Removing Egg

BROKEN EGGS AND EGG EATING

A cock bird is often destructive and breaks the eggs. The hen may also be guilty; turning the eggs she may damage one and the harm is then done the habit forms and many eggs are broken. Weak shells are a common cause of the problem lack of grit such as cuttlefish bone or oyster shell grit may be the root of the trouble. Examine the eggs and, if they appear "patchy", with little or no lustre on the shells, they are probably suffering from lack of calcium. The answer is to keep a plentiful supply available, particularly cuttlefish bone. Sometimes by accident a bird will crack an egg, taste the contents with her beak, and then become an egg eater. Such birds are a curse because they destroy all the work and effort put into a breeding season.

Possible preventive measures are as follows:

1. Remove the eggs quickly when laid and replace with dummy eggs.

2. Fill an egg with strong mustard and put sellotape over the holes. Once she has tasted the unsavoury mixture she should stop the habit.

3. Make sure that the birds have adequate water, minerals, greenstuff and seed.

4. Use specially designed nest box with allows an egg to drop through to a safe compartment.

UNRELIABLE MOTHER

Cannibalism and other obnoxious traits can exhibit themselves in birds without any warning. At times a young bird is involved and with maturity she will improve. Inadequate feeding, lack of water, poor accommodation and a variety of other factors may turn the hen into an unreliable breeder. Try changing the cock and move to an alternative aviary, thus eliminating possible causes.

BREEDING ROOM REGISTER

PEN No. . . . . COCK . . . . HEN . . . .

First Egg Laid	Hen Set	Due to Hatch	No. of Young	Remarks

PEN No. . . . . COCK . . . . HEN . . . .

First Egg Laid	Hen Set	Due to Hatch	No. of Young	Remarks

Register which shows all essentials for each hen

Constant interference with the nest box may cause desertion or other undesirable trait so try to be patient and restrict any viewing of eggs or chicks to once or twice at the most. Many hens resent any form of intrusion and become unsteady on the eggs, often being alarmed to the extent of deserting the eggs.

BREEDING RECORDS

It is at the start of the incubation and particularly the point at which the chicks are removed from their parents that records must be carefully kept, and this is especially true if the aim is to begin the establishment of a line. It will also be to the advantage of the breeder to know how the pair brought up their young, what problems were encountered, how many eggs were laid, how many were fertile or infertile, the quality of the chicks produced from any given pair in terms of size, type and feather quality and any other records which the breeder might decide are important to the continuance of the line.

Some breeders claim to be able to look into a flight of grown chicks and to be absolutely certain in asserting that a particular chick came from a particular pair. This is very difficult to believe, especially when many birds are concerned.

There is only one way to be absolutely sure on this point, and that is to place split celluloid rings on the legs of the chicks before separating from the parents; thus leaving no doubt about the parents. Rings are put on by the use of a fluted metal tool which is supplied by the ringmakers.

PROBLEMS IN THE BREEDING SEASON
Desertion

One problem which may be encountered is that of the hen deserting the nest. There are a variety of reasons for desertion, and one very common cause is the lack of an adequate supply of green food or fruit Another cause of desertion is lack of privacy for the sitting hens.

Nest boxes should not be placed too close to the windows of the bird room where the hens are presented with external distractions which may frighten them and cause them to leave the nest. Unusual noises both inside and outside the bird room should be completely eliminated during breeding operations and it would be true to say that there are many experienced fanciers who will not allow visitors into their bird rooms while breeding is in progress.

Another theory on the problems of desertion is that the birds are not being offered sufficient vitamin supplements. Whether this is true or not is a matter of debate.

Many fanciers believe that if the ordinary diet is well balanced the birds will obtain all the vitamins they require. Other breeders give vitamin supplements at breeding time in order to make sure that the birds have a good and regular supply.

As we have already noted, the weather may also play a part in causing the hens to desert their chicks.

ARTIFICIAL REARING

Parrot and Parrakeet chicks are quite small when hatched and are quite helpless so hand feeding is essential to development. There is obviously a relationship between the size of the parents and the chicks. Thus a mature Hyacinthnine Macaw is likely to be around 2.50 to 3.00k and the newly born chick will be around 21 g. In 10 weeks it will have grown to about 1.50 k which means a terrific input of food. Parrakeets are much smaller and therefore more difficult in the early stages.

The rate of growth in chicks is quite phenomenal and this is the trend in all species. However, these weights are not uniform and newly hatched chicks can vary tremendously even from the same species.

Thus in the case of Umbrella Cockatoos (*Cacatua alba*) it was found that 8 chicks were from 10.59 to 16g with the median of 12.5g.* The pair laid one or two eggs each time they nested, but would only feed one (the first) chick so the pair were removed and were hand fed.

In another case dusky lories it was found the parents were not feeding the two chicks and one died. The remaining chick was taken into the house and put into a hospital cage. It was fed by syringe containing honey and warm water. They hen introduced baby food *Milupa* and fed the chick every hour which was reduced to every two hours on the second day. The amount of food was 3 ml each time, but 4 ml in the morning. This was increased to 5ml a time when 10 days old and was doubled 6 days later and the down started to show. At 3 weeks of age the amount was about 16 ml and increasing. The period of feeding was now every five hours.

There was less dependence on the hospital cage and the bird was growing feathers. These two mini-case studies indicate what is involved. They show a devotion on the part of the bird keeper and a great deal of time spent, especially in the early stages.

Artificial Rearing has concentrated on the large expensive parrots and not on Parrakeets. One of the reasons is the need to have tame birds for pets which can be taught to speak and are handlked wthout difficulty. There is no theoretical reason that bars parrakeets being hand reared, but using the natural methods is regarded as being more acceptable, viewed from a practical point-of-view and, possibly, ethical considerations; some would argue that all types of parrots and parrakeets should be allowed to have a natural life and not constantly handled and kept in small cages.

Breeding Umbrella Cockatoos, **Ralph C Small, USA, in an article for** *The Parrot Society Magazine*, **October, 1980.**

Holding A Baby Parrot

PROCEDURES FOLLOWED

When the chicks are hatched by the mother then a decision must be made on what should be done, whether to allow natural methods to prevail or to take out of the nest and rear them artificially by hand feeding. Some breeders advocate taking all youngsters from birds which have not reared previously on the grounds that they may not have the experience and it would be safer to rear by hand. However, unless the bird is allowed to try then it will not be possible to ever know whether a pair will rear successfully.

If the species is in short supply and an attempt is being made to breed as many as possible to enlarge captive stock or to release some into the wild then a crash programme might be feasible. In this way, by removing the young, the birds will mate again and produce more eggs which they may hatch or, alternatively, may be placed in an incubator.

When the period of rearing is quite long, as is the case with the large parrots such as Macaws, then the chicks may be taken from the parents at a few weeks old and 'finished off' by hand feeding. With the quite small species the feeding of the chicks when a day old may be quite difficult and require very delicate handling so feeding by parents at the early stages may be advisable.

Warmth is absolutely vital to the newly hatched parrot, the requirement being in the region of 35⁰ C. (approaching 96⁰ F), but might be slightly plus or minus, so select a level which is comfortable for the chicks. As the chicks grow, the heat can be reduced gradually until they are fully feathered, when they will manage with normal room heat, although if in cold weather some heat may be required.

Various forms of heat sources have been tried, along with a thermostat, so the heat can be controlled. In poultry chick rearing, hovers and infrared lamps have been used quite successfully, the lamp being raised each day to gradually reduce the heat until the chicks are not requiring a high level.

There is therefore much experience available on rearing chicks relating to large poultry, bantams, pheasants, guinea fowl, turkeys and other related livestock. The main difference is that in these cases the chicks can eat themselves from 2 days so they will thrive and develop provided there is adequate heat, which is also a vital requirement for parrot chicks.

The brooders, methods of heating, weaning and other related requirements can therefore follow the types used for poultry chicks. Many parrot breeders have started from scratch not appreciating that incubation and rear-

Feeding Baby Parrot

ing goes back hundredsof years so the equipment available can be adapted for parrot chicks. It is therefore appropriate that some of the equipment should be looked at, and then adapted. Plastic boxes can be used for keeping individual chicks or a group from the same nest, and these can be placed in brooders which are the specific requirements. Notes are reproduced to show the principles and possibilities.

ARTIFICIAL BROODING

Artificial brooding infers the use of equipment which provides conditions similar to those of the brooding hen, but in much larger numbers.

Temperature Requirement

The optimum brooding temperature is between 35°C and 37.7°C measured at a height 5 cm above floor level. As the chicks grow and feather so the temperature requirement decreases. The following is a guide, according to weeks of age, for brooding temperatures:

Age in weeks	Temperature in° C
0 -I	32 -35
I -2	30 -32
2 -3	27 -30
3 -4	24 -27
4- 5	21 -24
5-6	18-21
6-7	15-18

The best guide to temperature requirement is the state of the chicks they are huddled around the heating unit the temperature is too low; they are widely spread out the temperature is too high. Chicks which are too hot or cold cheep plaintively. Contented chicks are those which eat regularly and appear contented.

BROODING EQUIPMENT

Manufacturers of brooding equipment usually provide instructions. These should be followed unless proved incorrect.

Heat for brooding can be supplied by electricity, gas, solid fuel, paraffin oil or hot water. Electricity is easy to operate and is clean, but in some areas the source is unreliable owing to voltage drops, power failures or breakdown of equipment. The greatest benefit is that it is clean and easily controlled. There are many types of electric brooders on the market, varying from infra-red lamps to heat storage brooders to large canopy types.

Types of brooder are many and varied, especially for those wishing to rear on a regular basis; thus:

1. Heated Box -- wood or plastic.

2. Hospital Cage -- available from pet food stores.

3. Brooders specially made, or adapted from brooders developed for poultry chicks.

4. Rearers on a single basis or in a block (Multiple Rearers) so that chicks can be raised through the different stages at the appropriate temperature level. Often each compartment is at a different heat level so gradually the chicks are hardened off by stages.

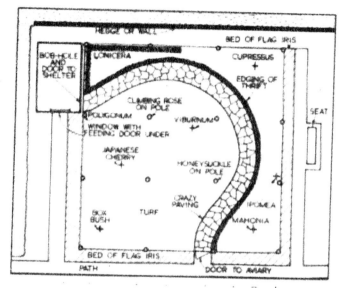

Aviary Which is Landscaped
From Aviaries -- A Practical Handbook.
Landscaping allows the birds to have natural surroundings and
gives a pleasing appearance in the garden.

FURTHER NOTES HAND REARING

Hand rearing is a very difficult and time consuming task, and although it would be true to say that chicks have been reared by hand, the chances of its succeeding were at one time very remote. However, there has been rapid progress in the techniques used so large numbers are reared by hand by professional rearers. There has to be a methodical approach with proper records, and within the system of management the following would be included:

1. Place rings or bands on chicks when old enough so a full record can be kept of breeding stock. Use the size appropriate for the species.

2. Have a special, well insulated room for rearing with adequate heat and ventilation and use a small incubator or rearer of the type used for poultry chicks, but on a smaller scale. Heated floor pads, infra-red lamps and even dull light bulbs may be used to get the correct temperature. The latter should be 99° F (37.2° C) for two days and then reduced to about 92° F at a week old and gradually down until, when feathers have appeared, very little heat will be required, provided room temperature is steady and adequate. The important requirement is just sufficient heat for them to be comfortable and active.

3. Use small plastic trays or boxes to hold the chicks, each chick being placed in a soft, strong tissue which acts as a cover at first and facilitates handling and hygiene. Each day the tissues are discarded, thus keeping the brooding container clean.

4. Use a high protein food. Bread and milk is popular, but vitamins and supplements should be added. In the USA they favour what they term Dog Chow (dog biscuit) which is mixed with creamed corn, garden vegetables, peanut butter and vitamins; the mixture must be very finely minced and some

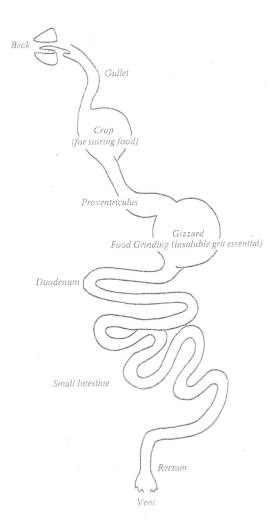

Beak

Gullet

Crop
(for storing food)

Proventriculus

Gizzard
Food Grinding *(insoluble grit essential)*

Duodenum

Small Intestine

Rectum

Vent

Digestive System of the Seed–eating Parrot
(Note: Grit is vital for grinding food in Gizzard)

breeders buy specially mixed baby food, although this is quite expensive.

ARTIFICIAL INCUBATION

NOTE: Some breeders who are producing large numbers of parrot chicks use artificial incubators, a practice hundred-of-years old for poultry and pheasants. These have been quite successful, but it does need time and skill to achieve good results. Moreover, there must be sufficient eggs being produced to make the venture worthwhile. Zoological gardens and specialist bird zoos such as Bird World, near Farnham, Surrey have been quite successful. The principles of incubation must be understood and applied to aviary birds; see for example, *Artificial Incubation & Rearing*, Joseph Batty, BPH, which applies mainly to gallinaceous birds, but applicable to parrots.

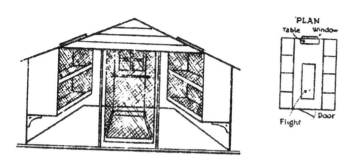

Plan for Multiple Compartment Aviary

Flight and Sleeping Section
Simple, yet quite effective.

CHAPTER 8

OBSERVATIONS
&
A CONCISE
CASE
STUDY

Modern Aviary
Ideal for Inside and, with the sides covered, may be used out-
side. Extra protection essential for inclement weather.
Suitable for one or two pairs of Kakarikis.

EXPERIENCE COUNTS

In writing about any aviary birds it should be appreciated that they are all individuals, just like humans, so they tend to behave differently and have various likes and dislikes.

They are affected by the environment in which they are bred and brought up. The latter is important because the habits acquired in the early stages will tend to remain with them and, although changes can be made, it may take many weeks for the full acceptance to come about.

FIRST PURCHASES

My first purchases of Kakarikis was around 1985 which were the normal Red-fronted type. The pair was kept in a small shed-cum-aviary about 2 metres long and 1.2 m. high and deep with a twil-weld netting on two-thurds of the front.

There was a roosting perch in the sleeping quarters and two perches, put long-ways in the flight. Kakarikis are always on the move and therefore must have plenty of opportunity to exercise by flying or running up and down the wire.

The nest box was the standard type illustrated earlier and there was no problem with acceptence. They bred and multiplied, when a much larger shed and flight were required.

Even when there were 20 or more living together there were no serious problems. It was obvious that some birds were dominant in their attitude, but there was no vicious behaviour, resulting in serious injuries. They were a happy family living in harmony.

As a result of this experience I came to the conclusion that Kakarikis will live together in harmony. I was wrong.

Possibly this behaviour was due primarily to the fact that they were all inter-related. Line breeding was practised, keeping to members of the family, but not too close. In fact, some degree of inbreeding was inevitable, but it did not result in any health problems. A measure to offset the possible effects was to build a second aviary so there could be switches over, when new blood was needed, which was also related.

The stock remained at the same size, fairly small.

A FRESH START

Due to moving to a smaller house with a small garden, previously having about 5 acres, the large collection of poultry, pigeons, parrots, and waterfowl, had to be sold off or given to friends. This is one of the penalties of growing older.

In 2005, having got settled in the new house, after visiting a local bird club meeting and sale, I decided to purchase a pair of Kakarikis which were a Splashed type, being primarily green, but with yellow patches covering about one third of the body.

These were quite large in size, about 50 per cent larger than the previous Kakarikis. Obviously, they had been selected for size and, possibly, the result of crossing with another strain, thus giving more vigour.

Another factor, which was not analysed further at the time, was the time breeding had been done. On enquiring whether the birds were a proven pair I was told 'Yes', and had last bred towards *the end of last year*; the sale was being held in April.

The only way the birds would have bred at the end of the year, in our climate, would be when heat and artificial light were provided. I experienced this situation when carrier pigeons* had to be moved to stables, which had electric lights, which were switched on in the evening. These stables were very well insulated with a special material, so no artficial heating was needed. Surprisingly, the pigeons bred at a rapid rate.

The birds purchased were placed in a small aviary which was quite high, with numerous perches. The sides were covered in a special perxpex to prevent wind and rain blowing in.

They settled down quite well, and took to the basic Parrot Mix which included a wide range of items, sunflower seeds, nuts, slices of dried bananas, some small dried peppers, various small seeds, and sweet corn and wheat. The largest proportion was sunflower seed. A problem was experienced with the ground nuts in shells, which large parrots enjoy, but Kakarikis find difficult to crack.

See *Carrier Pigeons*, Joseph Batty, BPH

Outside Aviary

This contains many natural perches and is large enough for the breeder to step inside.

A regular supply of fresh greens was given daily. These included grass clippings, clover, chickweed, dandelion, dock and lettuce.

They were not interested in apples or other fruit so, after a number of attempts, this was discontinued. Later birds liked apples.

Breeding

The cock bird went through the usual preliminaries for mating, flying around, rushing up to the hen and feeding her, and generally making a great display. However, at no time was he observed mounting the hen to copulate. It was assumed he was doing this early mornings or evenings.

Five eggs were laid in the nest box and incubation started. Unfortunately, there was a long wait. In the end, they were checked and broken open, only to find that they were quite clear, which indicated that the hen or the cock, was not performing. At that stage there was no indication which one, or both, had failed.

They made no attempt to breed again so the next possibility appeared to be next Spring. However, this was not to be, because at the first signs of very cold weather the hen died. She was found to be rather thin, although she had been feeding and there had been a permanent supply of fresh water.

This turned out to be a great disappointment because it was now fairly obvious that the birds had been kept indoors, with light and heat in cold weather. In such circumstances a seller has a duty to inform the new owner so appropriate shelter can be provided.

The age of the birds should also be revealed because those of a few years old may not survive a move to quite different surroundings. If the plan is to have an outside aviary, the previous management system should be known.

The food being given should also be known because turning to an entirely different menu may cause some distress. A Parrot Mix may not be acceptable when previously, a Parrakeet Mix was being used. Also supplementary foods should be known so they can be continued.

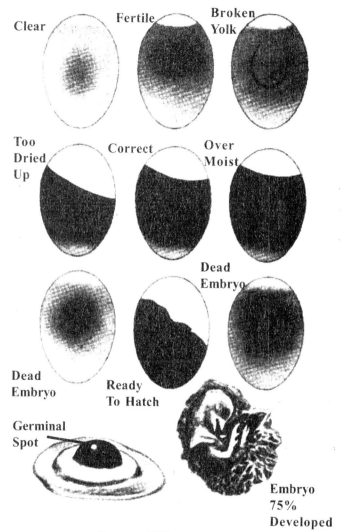

Eggs at Different Stages

These are not Kakariki Eggs, but the principles are the same. The top Air Space is an important indicator on correct incubation, show whether moisture content is correct. Incubation period is 20 days, similar to a bantam. Leave the nest at 4 - 5 weeks.

The cock managed to stand the cold weather, but he was rather subdued. Later, when new stock was introduced, he was quite boisterous and a young male that was placed in the aviary was chased around, and a new hen was taken over by the old cock.

Unfortunately, the supremacy did not last very long, possibly due to illness or old age, because within a few weeks, the new cock took over. Suddenly, the young bird realized he was stronger and attacked the older bird who fled. After that it was down hill all the way, the older bird being chased round the aviary and attacked in a vicious manner, until, in the end, he succumbed and died.

This modified my views, and generally accepted opinions, that Kakarikis are very docile. They are within the family Group, but introduce new stock and a different story emerges.

Had the person selling the stock been quite straight forward the unsuccessful period, including failure to produce fertile eggs, might have been avoided. Birds kept inside can be quite healthy, but turned out in winter in an exposed aviary can be a different matter.

The age of the birds is also an important question because, although those over two years of age can still breed, the older they are, the less likely the success, especially if they are placed in an entirely different situation.

This story led to the conclusion that purchases are best made from a breeder by visiting him and seeing first hand his birds. It will soon be apparent when viewed, which are the young birds, which will most likely breed, next season. Exposure to the weather can also be established, which is very important if the intention is to keep birds in an outside aviary.

Details of the food given can also be established. In fact, a breeder who wants to play fair will have a duplicated sheet showing the types of seed and other items provided.

Even the hoppers and drinkers being used is also useful knowledge because the birds are accustomed to these and something quite different might prove a set back.

ANOTHER START

As noted on the preceding page, the hen of the old stock died, which necessitated bringing in new birds, which caused problems in the initial stages.

When the old hen died new stock was purchased from a well kown breeder in London. Before deciding, an appointment was made for a visit.

We went by car and parked outside on the road. He had two buildings, taking up a substantial part of the back garden. Within the buildings there were separate flight pens where the birds were kept. A number of nest boxes hung from horizontal wires.

In one pen were the conventional Greens and Splashed Yellows. In the other were the Lutinos, a sparkling yellow, and very attractive. There were also some Greens which were used to keep the Lutinos a good, deep colour.

Two pairs were obtained, both Mutations, green and yellow splashed. One pair was placed in the original aviary with the old cock, who at first, bullied the newcomer, although, as noted, this did not last long because the young cock, once established, turned on the old bird, and killed him.

Breeding

After that the new pair mated the hen laid 6 eggs and hatched three of these; the other three were clear.

These were raised quite successfully and once they were feathered ventured outside the nest box. There were two, mainly green in colour, and one Cinnamon, which, unfortunately, got out of the aviary and escaped without any later sighting.

The youngsters settled down quickly and for about 10 days were fed by the male bird, until they learned to take the food themselves. They also became quite proficient in flying and running up the wires on the outer walls. At first it seemed they would never master flying from one perch to another, or taking off from the floor, but, in fact, within 2 - 3 weeks they were almost as flexible as the parents.

FEEDING

All are agreed that a *balanced diet* is important for the continued well being of the birds. Moreover, the food should be obtainable and fresh.

Study of the behaviour by siting the aviaries just outside the French window of the sitting room allowed regular observations to be made. This was in addition to the times watching the birds when in the garden and when feeding them or cleaning them out each weekend.

The following facts were revealed:

1. Birds become accustomed to being fed early in the morning and in the evening. They show this by looking in expectation and flying around, showing they know feeding and watering are about to take place,

2. If a bird bath is not provided they will use the open type stainless steel containers provided which hang on the side, within a special fitting. This means the water gets dirty quite quickly because wood savings are carried in on the feet. The alternative is to have a separate bird bath, which is better if space permits. *Kakarikis seem to want to splash water over themselves even in cold weather !*

3. There is more substance in the *Parrot Mix* obtainable from the food merchant, but there is also more waste. The birds break through the husks of the sunflower seed and after eating the kernel leave the outer shell which soon accumulates in the container. *Periodically it can be emptied on to the floor which allows the birds to scratch and forage.*

There is not as much waste with the *Parrakeet Mix.*

They are scratching birds, rather like bantams, so an open dish is recommended for the food. In fact, they seem to prefer going on the floor and scratching rather than using a normal food hopper.

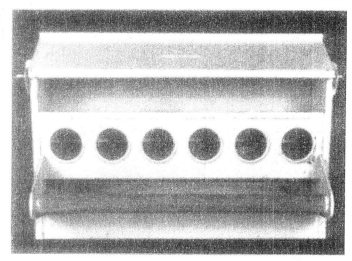

Conventional Seed Hopper
Not recommended for Kakarikis, which prefer to scratch.

Assorted Food Containers
Again not recommended for Kakarikis

4. A number of new foods were discovered by experiment:
(a) **Maize on the cob**. Stuck on a spike at the side of the flight will allow this corn on the cob to be eaten as fancied.

(b) **Celery** on a bulldog clip.
The outer parts can be used and the remainder kept for salads and other household uses.
These were welcome, one stick for a pair of birds, every other day. Each stick should be firmly secured in the clip, because if it falls on the floor the birds seem to lose interest.

(c) **Red pepper bases**. These are saved from the peppers used in the kitchen for cooking or salads. The base of each one is cut off, leaving the seeds intact.
The birds peck at the red part and take the inner seeds.

(d) **Carrots** whole placed in a spiral device used for hanging on the side of a rabbit hutch and normally used for rabbits.
Instead, one is hung inside the aviary and the carrot pushed in when it is held firmly in the wires until eaten. Clean, young carrots are soon eaten.

(e) **Seeds** not eaten can be thrown into a growing pot or on to the garden when they sprout and grow into plants. These can be pulled out when a reasonable size and fed to the birds, including the roots, which the birds like -- no doubt a source of calcium.

Various other possible foods are tried. Wholemeal bread freshly toasted (left-overs from breakfast) and be cut into halves and then placed in a bulldog clip.
Do not be too disappointed if certain foods are ignored. Fresh bananas and plums were not appreciated. Neither were the seeds of melons; possibly if they had been dried, they would have been more acceptable. Aviary birds do not appear to be as inbtellegent as poultry in trying out strange foods.
Remove any discarded food and throw it away before it goes mouldy.   —

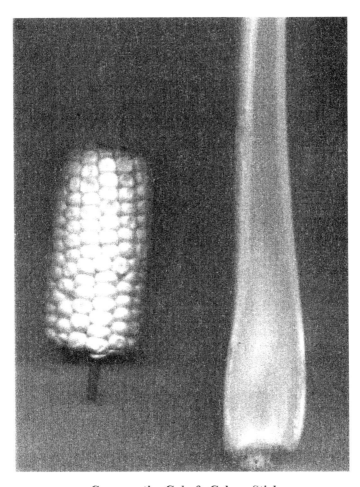

Corn-on-the-Cob & Celery Stick
Both proved to be very popular.

DETAILS OF BREEDING

6 th June three chicks hatched, and 3 clear.

15th June. Chicks beginning to attempt to sit up. Covered in light grey down. One was lighter in colour and turned out to be a Cinnamon mutation.

16th June. Hen staying off nest for long periods in the day time. Visited frequently to feed young.

23rd June. Hen off nest for most of the time, this making them 17 days old.
Two chicks showing quills in wings, but no colour. Third chick not as advanced.

NOTE: Observed pair mating on perch at about 7.00 am.

29th June. Chicks now sitting up. Colour now appearing; two green and the light grey down chick was a yellowy-green on wings and back.

6 th July. Feathers on back, almost covered. Head, breast, wings and tail showing signs, but no colour.

9th July. One chick appearing at pop hole and being fed by cock bird.

NOTE: Pair now copulating every few days. Hen visiting spare nest box each day, but no eggs. Eating much food, especially relishing celery stick placed in aviary daily.

15 th July. Feathering now completed, the front of the head being the last. Tails were rather bedraggled and not fully grown, due to being in nest.
First one emerged from the nest box and scrambled around, attempting to go up the wires of the aviary. Two remained in nest box until , but came out 21st July.

Aviaries When Different Species Are Kept

Now, after a few days scrambling around, could fly quite well. The Cinnamon, although small, went in the drinking pot, and bathed.

Gave them raspberry leaves which they apppeared to relish; continued with other foods listed earlier.

Unhappy Sequel

Although the hen laid eggs she never settled down to incubate them. No doubt the experience of the Aesop who stated:

Never count your chickens before they are hatched.

The Cinnamon appeared to be very tame and would allow me to touch her wing butt with my finger. Alas, I grew careless and she suddenly flew over my shoulder and outside to freedom.

From this experience I learned that immature birds cannot be trusted. When an adult bird escapes, especially when paired, it is only too pleased to return to the comfort of the aviary.

It may be caught by using a small net at the end of a cane, similar to those used by boys for fishing in a pond or at the sea-side. When it lands on the side, trying to find a way in, the capture is usually straight forward. Alternativly, drive the bird into the garden shed or green house and enter, closing the door, when catching the bird is easier.

INDEX

INDEX KAKARIKIS

(See also Index *Parrakeet Management)*

INDEX PARRAKEET MANAGEMENT
(See also Index *Kakarikis*)

INDEX PARRAKEET MANAGEMENT

INDEX (Cont)

INDEX (Cont)